hh'   H·E·Dobl

A DASH OF
SPICE

A DASH OF
SPICE

Spices for Beauty, Health & Cooking
 Recipes & Traditions

KATHRYN HAWKINS & GAIL DUFF

CHARTWELL
BOOKS, INC.

A QUARTO BOOK

Published by Chartwell Books
A Division of Book Sales, Inc.
114 Northfield Avenue
Edison, New Jersey 08837

This edition produced for sale in the U.S.A., its territories
and dependencies only.

Reprinted 2003

ISBN 0-7858-1724-7

This book was designed and produced by
Quarto Publishing plc
The Old Brewery
6 Blundell Street
London N7 9BH

Editor: Cathy Marriott
Senior Art Editor: Elizabeth Healey
Assistant Editor: Judith Evans
Copy Editors: Mary Senechal, Deborah Savage
Designer: Allan Mole
Picture Researcher: Zoë Holtermann
Photographer: Juliette Piddington
Illustrator: Valerie Hill
Art Director: Moira Clinch
Assistant Art Director: Penny Cobb
Editorial Director: Pippa Rubinstein

Typeset in Great Britain by Central Southern Typesetters, Eastbourne
Manufactured in Hong Kong by Regent Publishing Services Ltd
Printed in China by Leefung-Asco Printers Ltd

CONTENTS

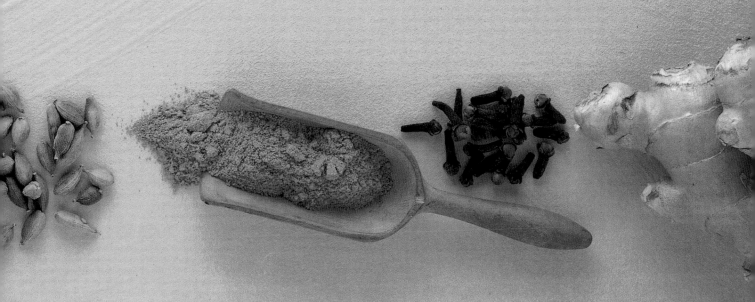

INTRODUCTION

SPICE—THE VERY WORD CONJURES UP VISIONS OF SPANISH GALLEONS IN FULL SAIL, PIRACY ON THE HIGH SEAS, TREACHERY IN FAR-FLUNG LANDS, EXOTIC SCENTS, DELICIOUS FLAVORS, AND LUXURY FOODS. SPICES HAVE BEEN PURSUED AND FOUGHT OVER, AND MANY HAVE COMMANDED HIGH PRICES.

Boats called caravels once traveled along the old spice routes.

Loading boxes of spices onto bullock carts in India in the late 19th century, for transporting to the nearest railroad station. From there they traveled to ports for export abroad.

What exactly is a spice and what makes it different from a herb? The main distinction lies in the part of the plant that is used. Herbs are generally leaves. Spices can be flower buds, such as cloves; fruits, such as pepper, capsicum peppers, allspice, nutmeg, and vanilla; seeds, such as anise, caraway, cardamom, coriander, and mustard; or rhizomes that spread underground, such as those of ginger and turmeric. Saffron, which is in a class of its own, consists of the stigmas of a crocus plant.

Spices can grow on herbaceous plants, such as anise or caraway, whose leaves are also harvested, or on small, leafy plants, such as those of the capsicum genus, which are grown only for their fruits. Ginger and turmeric plants resemble large lilies; pepper and vanilla are vine plants; and cloves, nutmeg, and mace grow on trees.

Some spices, such as caraway, coriander, cumin, and anise, can, with care, be grown in gardens and plots in temperate climates, but the rest need special conditions. Pepper, cloves, cinnamon, nutmeg, mace, cardamom, ginger, and turmeric all originate in the tropical

area of Asia between the latitudes 25°N and 10°S of the Equator, where the climate is warm and humid. Allspice, vanilla, and capsicum peppers come from the American tropics. Spices have traveled within these tropical areas and also through the same latitudes in Africa, but it is impossible to grow many of them elsewhere.

For this reason, the exotic spices have always been far more expensive than herbs. Whereas herbs can be grown on one's own windowsill, most people in the world have always had to buy spices, and the journey from the place of origin to the market is in most cases, even now, a long one.

The route begins on a plantation somewhere in the tropics, where the trees or plants are cultivated. At precisely the right moment the buds, seeds, or fruits are picked by hand. They then go through drying and sometimes curing processes, also mainly done by hand, before being packed and conveyed to a port or airport for export.

In times gone by, spices were transported by sea in dug-out canoes and other wooden vessels, and overland along the old spice routes, carried by packhorse, donkey, and

Spikenard and saffron; calamus and cinnamon, with all the trees of frankincense; myrrh and aloes, with all the chief spices ... Awake, O North Wind; and come thou south; blow upon my garden, that the spices thereof may flow out, let my beloved come to his garden, and eat his pleasant fruits.

SONG OF SOLOMON 4:14–16

Jolly Red Nose

Nose, nose, nose, nose!
And who gave thee this jolly red nose?
Nutmegs and ginger, cinnamon and
cloves,
And they gave me this jolly red nose.

THOMAS RAVENSCROFT, *DEUTEROMELIA*, 1609

In medieval times, Venice was the center of the spice trade.

camel. They passed through cities whose names still stir the imagination: Rhambacia, Persepolis and Charax, Kashgar, Marib, Yathrib and Petra. The travelers had true tales to tell and yarns to spin, and who would not pay over the odds for a stale nutmeg when it came laden with all the romance of the mystic East?

Down the centuries different countries dominated the spice trade, making as much as they could out of both producers and buyers, but nevertheless putting their own lives and properties at risk in what was essentially a hazardous investment. If your ship came home, you were indeed fortunate, but if it foundered at sea, you had lost everything. The Phoenicians were the first spice traders, followed by the Arabs, the Venetians, the Portuguese, the Dutch, the British, and the Americans. Today spices are exported by the countries that produce them.

Why the great desire for spices? Besides being exotic and mysterious, they were, and still are, a highly versatile commodity. They have been used for flavoring and preserving food; for making cosmetics, perfumes, and toiletries; for scenting rooms; and in the preparation of medicines and preventives of all sorts. The fragrance of spices is warm, sweet, and complex, and spices always impart a subtle richness to the dishes they are used in.

Among the age-old uses of spices is the scenting of cosmetics. A Roman woman would have an elaborate beauty ritual: here she admires herself in the mirror probably after having a fragrant bath and a massage with perfumed oils.

THE STORY OF SPICE

FOR PERHAPS AS LONG AS 9,000 YEARS SPICES HAVE BEEN HARVESTED TO ENHANCE PEOPLE'S DIET, IMPROVE THEIR HEALTH, GIVE THEM PLEASANTLY SCENTED SURROUNDINGS, AND MAKE THEM BEAUTIFUL.

Spices have been gathered in the wild and grown in plantations. They have been sought for and fought for; they have brought wealth to some and disaster to others; and greed for them helped to open up the trading routes of the world.

Nine thousand years ago, the hot red pepper we know by the Mexican name of chili was being gathered in South America. By 7,000 years ago (5000 B.C.) chilies were being cultivated. Around 3000 B.C. turmeric, cardamom, pepper, and mustard were grown in India, and mustard in China. Soon after, ginger and cinnamon arrived in both countries from the damp, tropical forests of Southeast Asia.

Spices were familiar in Egypt from at least 2500 B.C. The embalming industry used cumin, anise, and cinnamon. Other spices were mixed into cosmetics, room scents, incense, and food. Cinnamon and cassia came from what was known as the Land of Punt (present-day Somalia), and were traded for trinkets carried there by Egyptian sailors. Egypt was also supplied by another ancient spice route, which led up the west coast of India, either at the mouth of the Persian Gulf or farther south, then along the Arabian coast and finally through the Red Sea to Egypt

There are numerous mentions of spices in the Bible, both in the Old and New Testaments. In Ezekiel, the land of Phoenicia is described as having cassia and calamus (a dried aromatic root) in its markets; Moses used myrrh, cinnamon, and calamus in the anointing oil for the Ark of the Covenant; and Joseph of the coat of many colors was sold to a camel train carrying "spicery, gold and myrrh." The visit of the Queen of Sheba to Solomon in 950 B.C. was mainly to help promote the trade in spices between

Alexander the Great founded the city of Alexandria in Egypt, in 331 B.C. It later became an important spice-trading center.

The ancient Egyptians used spices for embalming animals as well as humans. The leg of mutton and the calf's head in a chest of papyrus leaves, shown here, were offerings to the gods.

their two countries. Much later, in the time of Jesus, the Pharisees paid their tithes in cumin, and Jesus himself told the parable of the mustard seed.

FROM B.C. TO A.D.

The Greeks and the Romans were great users of spices. They grew caraway, cardamom, anise, mustard, and fennel, and imported pepper, cassia, cinnamon, and ginger, which, in about 350 B.C., came in along the old silk road between India and the Mediterranean. Founded by Alexander the Great (356–323 B.C.), the city of Alexandria in Egypt became an important spice trading center.

Phoenician traders carried cinnamon and cassia to Greece, and spread rumors about the sources of cinnamon to protect their interests and drive up prices. Cinnamon grew in dangerous African swamps, they said, which were infested by ferocious batlike animals. The

The 394-foot high lighthouse at Alexandria was one of the Seven Wonders of the World. Its light would have guided the spice ships into port.

Phoenicians also traded in saffron, taking it, so legend has it, as far as Cornwall, in England.

During the second and first millennia B.C. the Arabs dominated the spice trade and, like the Phoenicians, propagated stories about their goods. Their version of the origins of cinnamon, for example, was that it was carried by giant birds to mountains in the north of Arabia, where their nests were attached by mud to steep cliffs. The only way to get the nests down was to lay a bait of large pieces of donkey meat for the birds to take up to the nests, which subsequently collapsed under the weight. In about the 1st century A.D., however, the Romans

An Arabian manuscript from 1222 showing two traders grinding spices.

Spicy Stories

In 450 B.C. Herodotus described the collecting of cassia and cinnamon, as told to him by Arab traders.

Cassia: *When the Arabians go out collecting cassia, they cover their bodies and faces, all but their eyes, with ox-hides and other skins. The plant grows in a shallow lake which, together with the ground round about it, is infested by winged creatures like bats. They have to be kept from attacking the men's eyes while they are cutting the cassia.*

Cinnamon: *What they say is that dry sticks … are brought by large birds, which carry them to their nests made of mud, on mountain precipices, which no man can climb, and that the method the Arabians have invented for getting hold of them is to cut up the bodies of dead oxen, or donkeys, or other large animals into joints, which they carry to the spot in question and leave on the ground near the nests. They then retire to a safe distance and the birds fly down and carry off the joints of meat into their nests, which, not being strong enough to bear the weight, break and fall to the ground. Then the men come along and pick up the cinnamon, which is subsequently exported to other countries.*

HERODOTUS, *HISTORY*, C.450 B.C.

9

began questing for spices themselves, even though the journeys were long and dangerous, beginning with a voyage along the Malabar coast of southwest India in search of pepper. Nevertheless, Arab domination persisted, and was reinforced after the founding of the Mohammedan empire in the 8th century.

In A.D. 40, a Greek named Hippalos discovered how to take advantage of the monsoon winds in the Indian Ocean to speed up sea voyages. The Romans also employed this knowledge, enabling them to break the Arab monopoly. Cinnamon from Sri Lanka (called Ceylon at this time) and pepper from India found their way to Rome. Pepper was the most used spice, and in A.D. 92 special pepper warehouses were built, called *horrea piperataria*. In A.D. 330 the Emperor Constantine founded the city of Constantinople, which became the center of the spice trade, and around this time cloves and nutmegs grown in the Moluccas in southeast Asia first found their way to the West.

The adventurer Marco Polo was the first European to discover the wealth of spices that were produced in the Far East.

In western Europe in the 16th century, spices were sold at markets and fairs, and from open-fronted stores like these in Paris.

The Romans took spices all over their empire, even to Britain, the farthest outpost; but as Rome fell to barbarian tribes, their trade was gradually blocked. In A.D. 408, they paid Alaric the Visigoth 3,000 lb. of pepper, plus silver, gold, skins, and silks, to raise the blockade on Rome. Alaric took the ransom—but two years later he also took the city.

AFTER THE ROMANS
The taste for spices continued unabated, although more northerly European countries, such as Britain, relied mainly on those that could be home-grown, plus pepper. This arrived chiefly as a gift to kings and the nobility, and was also paid in duties. In A.D. 982, King Aethelred II imposed extra Christmas and Easter tolls of pepper on German ships coming up to London Bridge to trade.

The Vikings took cardamom from Constantinople to Scandinavia, and it soon became their favorite spice. Ginger came to Germany and France in the 9th century and to Britain in the 10th. Saffron was grown in Britain, and caraway became naturalized in many parts of Europe. Mustard was another spice that could be home-grown in temperate climates. It was grown throughout Europe.

MEDIEVAL TIMES
There was a huge increase in the use of spices in medieval times. Pepper and ginger were the cheapest. They were sold at fairs and used by everyone except the poorest. The exotic spices were bought by wealthy city-dwellers. Because they were expensive, they were kept under lock and key and only released in carefully controlled quantities when needed.

It was probably the Crusades that brought spices to everyone's attention and, as the standard of living improved all over Europe, the demand for them became great. In 1204, Venetian ships plundered Constantinople and brought back enough wealth in spices to establish Venice at the center of the spice trade. When Marco Polo returned to Italy in 1297 with tales of spices in the Far East, people determined to reach these sources by sea. From then on, Europe entered the spice trade in earnest. The Venetians passed a law stating that all spices from the East had to pass through Venice, and the search for spice routes began. It was the beginning of the end of Arab domination of the spice trade.

10

OPENING UP THE WORLD

IT WAS MAINLY BECAUSE OF THE DESIRE FOR SPICES THAT THE EARLY EXPLORERS SET OUT IN SEARCH OF ROUTES AROUND THE WORLD. HERE IS A SUMMARY OF THE STORY OF EXPLORATION AND RIVALRY THAT SPANNED ALMOST 400 YEARS BEFORE SPICES BECAME WIDELY AVAILABLE.

During the 16th century, when this map was drawn, explorers were gradually adding to the knowledge of world geography.

Ferdinand Magellan set out from Spain in 1519 to reach the Spice Islands. He was killed in the Philippines, but one of his ships returned in 1522 with a valuable cargo of spices.

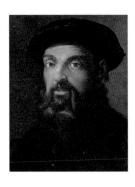

1471 The Portuguese crossed the Equator.
1486 Bartholomew Diaz sailed around the Cape of Good Hope.
1492 Columbus set out from Spain, reached San Salvador in the Bahamas and discovered hot red peppers in Cuba (Santa Domingo).
1493 Columbus, on his second voyage, found paprika being used to flavor local dishes in the West Indian island of Hispaniola.
1497 Vasco da Gama sailed around the Cape of Good Hope to Malabariu, India. He returned with cinnamon, cloves, ginger, pepper, and precious stones.
1509 The Spanish found allspice in Jamaica.
1511–14 The Portuguese gained control of the Malabar coast, Java, and Sumatra, and captured the Moluccan nutmeg trade.
1519 Ferdinand Magellan found nutmegs on the Indonesian island of Tidore.
1522 Only one of Magellan's ships returned, but it brought back a large cargo of nutmeg, mace, cinnamon, and sandalwood.
1536 The Portuguese occupied Ceylon.
1579 Cloves were taken back to Elizabeth I by Sir Francis Drake.
16th–17th centuries Ginger plantations were successfully established by the Spanish in the West Indies. The Dutch began to prosper as they supplied many ships to other countries.

1599 The English formed the East India Company to break the the Portuguese and Dutch monopoly which had increased pepper prices.
1602 The Dutch East India Company was founded to develop a Dutch empire in Asia.
1605–21 The Dutch drove the Portuguese out of the Spice Islands.
1636 The Dutch captured Sri Lanka.
1651 The Dutch now controlled the clove, nutmeg, and cinnamon trade and, for the next 100 or more years, they imposed a death sentence on anyone else who dared to plant spices.
1770 Pierre Poivre, the French administrator of Mauritius, smuggled clove, nutmeg, and cinnamon plants out of the Spice Islands and established plantations in Réunion, the Seychelles, and other French colonies.
1776 The first French cloves were harvested and plants were sent to English colonies.
1795 The first commercial pepper voyage set

This is the so-called Armada Portrait *of Elizabeth I. Encouraged by her, the British joined the race for spices in the late 16th century.*

out from Salem in the United States. After that, Boston, Portsmouth, Bath, and New London all became spice ports.
1824 The Dutch and British signed a treaty dividing up the spice areas between them.
1835 Vanilla was first grown in India.
1843 Nutmeg was planted on Grenada, which still calls itself the "nutmeg isle."

11

LORE AND LEGEND OF SPICES

INGREDIENTS OF APHRODISIACS AND LOVE POTIONS, PROTECTIONS AGAINST EVIL, SYMBOLS OF CHARACTER, COMFORTS FOR THE BEREAVED, GOOD-LUCK CHARMS, AND COMPONENTS OF INCENSE AND HOLY OIL: SPICES HAVE BEEN ALL THESE THINGS.

In William Shakespeare's A Midsummer Night's Dream, the mischievous spirit Puck puts a love potion into Titania's eyes while she is asleep to make her fall in love with the ass-headed Bottom. This 19th-century colored engraving is called Titania Sleeps *(far right).*

In his great work of anthropology *The Golden Bough*, George Frazer noted that the clove trees of the Molucca Islands were treated like pregnant women. No one was allowed to make a noise near them or to carry light or fire past them at night. It was also forbidden for a man to approach them wearing a hat. These precautions prevented the tree from being scared into dropping its fruit early, like a woman who had been frightened during her pregnancy.

LOVE POTIONS AND APHRODISIACS

The warming, sensuous fragrance of spices led people to believe that spices must have aphrodisiac qualities. Spices were also put into love potions, or love philters, which were said to induce people to fall in love. Aniseed, cardamom, cinnamon, nutmeg, mace, and ginger have been the main candidates for inclusion in aphrodisiacs. Greek and Roman courtesans, however, used a mixture of pepper, myrrh, and equal quantities of two scents called Cyprus and Egyptian, which was drunk from cups made of scented earthenware.

Coriander and dill in love potions were said to fill the person who drank them with desire, especially if the coriander was picked in the last quarter of the moon. The seeds could be burned as an incense, put into sweet dishes, or carried in a love sachet. A bath scented with dill seeds was believed to draw your lover to you,

A Spanish gypsy boils up a brew. Cauldrons were once in general use, but now they are associated with magic potions.

and so would chewing caraway seeds, alone or in a cake, or wearing a small pouch of caraway around the neck. Adding a small amount of vanilla sugar to love potions was reputed to make them more effective.

Caraway and cumin in love potions were thought to prevent lovers from being fickle. Cinnamon also had a reputation for keeping lovers faithful, especially if the plant from which the seeds were taken was cursed during sowing. Two red peppers, tied together, were placed under the pillow to keep a partner from straying, and European gypsies used pimientos in love spells.

In Germany it was a custom for the bride and groom to carry cumin, dill, and salt in their pockets during the wedding to guarantee faithfulness. In other parts of Europe, a young man leaving home for the army would take with him a cumin-flavored loaf baked by his sweetheart, after they had shared a glass of cumin-flavored wine. Turmeric was the good-luck spice at weddings in India, and Hindu brides were painted with it.

Cardamom, cloves, and cinnamon featured in a Persian recipe for regaining the affections of an errant husband. The spices were placed in a jar and a certain chapter of the Koran was read over them seven times backward. The jar was then filled with rosewater and left for a time. The husband's shirt was steeped in the resulting liquid, together with a piece of paper bearing his name and the names of four angels. Everything was then heated over the fire and, as the mixture boiled, the husband would begin to return.

SYMBOLS OF CHARACTER

Both the Greeks and the Romans regarded cumin seeds as a symbol of greed and miserliness. The Roman emperor Antoninus Pius, who lived in the 1st century A.D., spent so little on his social life that he was nicknamed "the cumin." He did, however, care more for the welfare of his subjects than most other emperors. Caraway was seen as a symbol of loyalty in England, where caraway cakes were served at harvest time to bind a worker's loyalty to the farm and his employers.

A coin depicting one of the signs of the zodiac, minted at the time of Antoninus Pius (A.D. 86–161).

The Roman Emperor Antoninus Pius, who was such a miser that his people nicknamed him "the cumin." Cumin, to the Romans, was a symbol of greed and parsimony.

An Arabian Love Philter

In the story of Ala-al-Din Abu-al in The Book of the Thousand Nights and One Night, *a love potion was prepared for the merchant Sham-al-Din:*

[the druggist] betook himself to a hashish seller, of whom he bought two ounces of concentrated Roumi opium and equal parts of Chinese cubebs [peppery berries], cinnamon, cloves, cardamoms, ginger, white pepper and mountain shiek [a kind of lizard]; and pounding them all together boiled them in sweet olive oil; after which he added three ounces of male frankincense in fragments and a cupful of coriander seed, and macerating the whole made it into an electuary with Roumi bee-honey. Then he put the confection in the bowl and carried it to the merchant, saying: 'Take of my electuary with a spoon after supping, and wash it down with a sherbet made of rose conserve; but first sup off mutton and house pigeon plentifully seasoned and hotly spiced.'

THE BOOK OF THE THOUSAND NIGHTS AND ONE NIGHT, TRANSLATED FROM THE ARABIC BY CAPTAIN SIR RICHARD BURTON, 1894

 17th-century artist's impression of a witch's gathering. Pepper, caraway, and fennel were once carried to avert what was known as "the evil eye" of a witch.

PROTECTION

In Britain, generally it was thought any object containing caraway could never be stolen and that if an attempt was made to take it away, the thief would remain a prisoner in the invaded house until he or she was discovered. In Germany, cumin was credited with the same powers. If it was put into bread, for example, it prevented the wood spirits from stealing the loaves.

Dill was believed to hinder witches, although it was also one of the herbs that witches used. A sachet of dill seeds used to be placed in the cradle to protect babies from evil influences. Pepper and caraway and fennel seeds were said to keep evil forces away from anyone who wore them in a pouch around the neck. Caraway and pepper were also reputed to ward off feelings of negativity. Peppercorns were mixed with salt and scattered round the house to keep out negative influences.

The Bible tells how a juniper tree protected Elijah from the persecutions of Ahab and this led to its being regarded throughout Europe as a symbol of protection. Juniper berries were considered a safeguard against evil spirits, and sprigs of juniper were hung over doors.

Turmeric was worn as an amulet in India and nutmegs have long been carried as good-luck charms. In Britain and the United States practitioners of natural magic believed nutmegs, star anise, and tonka beans, strung together, were a very potent form of protection. Star anise was carried as a general luck-bringer. Nightmares were kept away by slipping a small sachet of anise seeds under the pillow.

The legendary phoenix was believed to collect cinnamon, spikenard, and myrrh to fuel the fire in which it would cremate itself to become magically reborn (far right).

EVIL SPIRITS AND GHOSTS

In Bengal, ghosts and evil spirits were reputed to be unable to abide the scent of charred turmeric, and a piece of the burning root was waved in front of a person believed to be possessed by a tree spirit, so the spirit would depart. In medieval England, on the other hand, it was believed that burning together coriander, fennel seed, parsley, hemlock, liquor of black poppy, sandalwood, and henbane would produce a whole army of demons.

LIFE, DEATH, AND IMMORTALITY

In ancient China, cassia was regarded as the Tree of Life, which had flourished since the beginning of time in Paradise, a beautiful garden at the source of the yellow river. Whoever entered the garden and ate the fruit of the tree would live forever in eternal bliss. Another Chinese belief was that coriander would make anyone who consumed it immortal.

To ensure an easy delivery, pregnant women in Persia (now Iran) once wore a ball of saffron at the pit of their stomach. In the Molucca Islands, it was the custom to plant a clove tree for every child who was born, and it was believed that the fate of the tree was bound up with that of the child. In the United States, Britain, and throughout Europe cloves have also been carried by the bereaved in a small pouch around the neck, to bring comfort. In India, turmeric was regarded as a lucky charm for a newborn baby. A piece of the root was hung around a baby's neck, or turmeric

14

Tablets for a Love Potion

Take cinnamon, ginger, pepper, cress seed, rocket seed, mustard seed, of each half a drachm; bird's tongue, onion seed, crocodile, of each one scruple; white sugar dissolved in rose water, four ounces. Make into tablets.

WECHER, *EIGHTEEN BOOKS OF THE SECRETS OF ART AND NATURE* (UNDATED)

A 19th-century hand-colored woodcut showing an Egyptian priest and his scribe on the steps of a temple, where spiced incense would have been in frequent use.

water was regularly dabbed on its head until it had learned to walk.

BIRDS, REAL AND IMAGINED
In Britain caraway seeds were given to chickens and pigeons to prevent them from straying, and a piece of baked caraway dough was put into dovecotes for the same reason. On a more romantic level, the mythical phoenix was believed to collect cinnamon, spikenard, and myrrh to fuel the magic fire in which it would cremate itself and from which it would be magically reborn.

THE LEGEND OF SAFFRON
In Greek legend, a beautiful young man named Crocus was playing at quoits in a field with Mercury, messenger of the gods. A quoit thrown by Mercury hit Crocus on the head and killed him. When his friends grieved for him, saffron crocuses sprang up in the grass where his blood had fallen.

INCENSE AND HOLY OIL
The burning of incense made from spices, herbs and resins not only purifies the air and fumigates rooms, but has also been vested with magical significance. Cinnamon and mace have been burned to stimulate psychic powers; cloves to prevent gossip; and cumin for protection. The ancient Egyptians kindled incense to the sun god Ra three times a day: resin at sunrise, myrrh at midday, and kyphi, a mixture of spices and herbs, as the sun went down.

Burning kyphi was said to ensure peace and happiness to the household during the coming night and to bring pleasant dreams.

Scented oils have a history of use in religious ceremonies, for anointing both people and objects. In Exodus 30 it is written: "Take also unto thee principal spices, of pure myrrh five hundred shekels, and of sweet cinnamon half so much, even two-hundred-and-fifty shekels, and of sweet calamus two-hundred-and-fifty shekels, and of cassia five hundred shekels, after the shekel of the sanctuary, and of olive oil an hin [about 5 quarts]. And thou shalt make it an oil of holy ointment, an ointment compound after the art of the apothecary; it shall be an holy anointing oil."

15

This beautiful miniature Egyptian pyramid bears the image of the sun god Ra, for whom three different kinds of incense were burned during the day.

Spices for Health and Beauty

SINCE THE EARLIEST CIVILISATIONS SPICES HAVE BEEN USED TO MAINTAIN HEALTH, CURE DISEASE, AND SCENT CLOTHING AND ROOMS. THEY HAVE ALSO BEEN ESSENTIAL INGREDIENTS IN PERFUMES AND BEAUTY PREPARATIONS.

People have always been preoccupied with their stomachs, and spices have helped to enhance the diet as well as countering the effects of overindulgence or of eating food that is too rich. In Roman times, a cake called *mustacae*, heavily spiced with anise and cumin, was often served as a digestive at the end of a heavy meal. Similarly, the caraway cakes that were popular over the centuries in England and the caraway breads of Eastern Europe have been regarded as digestive aids as well as tasty foods. Caraway tea and fennel tea, made by pouring boiling water over the crushed seeds, are still used for this purpose.

Anise, caraway, dill, and coriander are age-old cures for flatulence. In the 1st century A.D. the Greek physician Dioscorides recommended dill to treat wind in babies, a remedy repeated by an English herbalist called Bancke, in his book *Bancke's Herbal*, in 1550 and still used. In 1597 John Gerard advised: "Anise helpeth the yeoxing or hicket [hiccups]." A tea of juniper berries has served digestive purposes in England, while in India turmeric is a digestive spice. On the other hand, if a lack of appetite is the problem, chili, ginger, and pepper in your food will encourage the desire to eat and stimulate the digestive juices.

SPICES FOR ACHES, PAINS, AND BRUISES

The comforting and warming effect of many spices has made them a remedy for countless aches and pains. In China, star anise was a rheumatism cure, and in Europe mustard plasters and embrocations of cinnamon and juniper were treatments for affected limbs. Chili oil has been an ingredient in ointments to rub on aching muscles, and mustard baths have soothed aching feet (see page 21). For bruises, Nicolas Culpeper, in 1640, recommended a caraway seed poultice: "The powder of the seed put into a poultice taketh away black and blue spots of blows and bruises."

SPICES FOR COLDS, COUGHS, AND INFLUENZA

Nothing will cure a cold, but its effects can be eased and soothed. A gargle with cardamom or turmeric tea has been known to relieve a sore throat, and in India, turmeric tea is also drunk to counter cold symptoms. Infusions of ginger and cayenne (see page 21) can be effective. Culpeper advised taking black mustard seed for colds: "It purges the brain by sneezing, and draws down the rheum and other viscous humours, and with some honey added it is good for coughs." If that sounds unpalatable, you can always put your feet in a mustard bath.

For chest complaints, a juniper infusion was often recommended, and allspice oil has often been used in a massage oil for asthma. John Gerard, in 1597, recommended cumin: "Being taken in a supping broth it is good for the chest and cold lungs." Infusions of cayenne

Buttermilk and Fennel Seed Skin Cleanser

This is an excellent cleanser for oily skin. Fennel is a strong astringent and should not be used for normal or dry skins.

⅔ cup buttermilk
1 tbsp fennel seeds

Put the buttermilk and fennel seeds into a double boiler and heat them gently for 30 minutes. Cool and leave to stand for 2 hours. Strain.
Pour the buttermilk into a clean, sterilized jar. Store it in the refrigerator for up to 2 weeks.

16

Nicholas Culpeper, (1616–54) was a practicing apothecary in the Spitalfields area of London. His herbal, The English Physician, *detailed the medicinal uses of numerous spices and herbs.*

An advertisement from the 1920s for Grossmith's spiced and fragrant Oriental Face Powder.

A plague doctor in Rome in the 17th century, wearing the sinister-looking leather "beak," which was stuffed with spices to keep infection at bay.

Honey Water

This is a variation of the recipe created by George Wilson, apothecary to James II (1685–88) of England. It makes a refreshing and soothing aftershave.

*1 tbsp honey
½ cup hot water
½ cup orange-flower water
4 tbsp vodka
4 drops coriander oil
4 drops musk oil
4 drops juniper oil
4 drops vanilla oil*

Put the honey into a large jug and pour the hot water over. Stir until the honey has dissolved. Leave until quite cold. Add the orange-flower water, vodka, and essential oils.
Pour the water through a funnel into a dark bottle.
Cover and shake well.

17

pepper and coriander and poultices of white mustard, bread crumbs, and vinegar have been prescribed for fevers.

SPICES FOR TOOTHACHE AND EARACHE

Clove oil is the spice remedy that usually comes to mind in connection with toothache but, although cloves are a mild antiseptic, the concentrated oil is an irritant and should be used with care. The Chinese use an infusion of cloves as a mouthwash, which is much more gentle. In India, burnt turmeric was once added to tooth powders to relieve dental troubles. An old-fashioned poultice for earache was made from caraway seeds pounded with the crumb of a hot new loaf.

SPICES TO CALM THE NERVES

Infusions made from anise, star anise, caraway, dill, and coriander are said to help calm the nerves. Saffron

was once a favorite European sedative, rendered more potent in the 18th and 19th centuries by being mixed with opium and canary wine.

SPICES AS PREVENTIVES

Spices have a mild antiseptic quality which was recognized many centuries ago. As a result, they have been used in a number of ways to counteract infection, particularly in times of plague. In medieval and Tudor times in Britain, many rich people carried silver pomanders containing aromatic mixtures of spices and resins, which could be held to the nose when the owners were traveling through an unsavory or infected district, or when they came into contact with poor people or plague sufferers.

In Venice, in the 17th century, plague doctors wore beaklike leather masks stuffed with spices to ward off infection. The first person to carry an orange stuck with cloves was Cardinal Wolsey, in 16th-century England. He took it with him when he visited his parishioners. The

In the bitterly cold conditions experienced by Napoleon's armies as they retreated from Russia in 1812, soldiers stuffed their boots with allspice berries to try to prevent chilblains.

18

"Vinegar of the Four Thieves," made by steeping spices and herbs in vinegar for three weeks, was said to have been used during a plague in Toulouse in 1720 by four robbers, who plundered the houses of plague victims without themselves becoming infected. Spices have also been burned in open pans called chafing dishes to fumigate houses in times of sickness. To prevent chilblains and other effects of the cold during the Napoleonic War in 1812, Russian soldiers put allspice berries in their boots.

A Victorian lady with sweet-smelling breath. Traditionally, clove, cinnamon, and anise oils have been added to toothpaste

SPICES FOR SWEET FLAVORS AND BREATH

Many of the medicines we take today would be totally unpalatable if it were not for the addition of small amounts of spice oils, such as cinnamon and juniper. Clove, cinnamon, and anise oils are added to tooth-pastes for flavoring. An infusion made from any of these can be used as a breath-freshening mouthwash: "Anise maketh the breath sweeter," said Turner's *Herbal* in 1551. Chewing cardamom seeds sweetens the breath and removes the smell of alcohol. After a meal in India, it is the custom to chew on a mixture of areca nut, lime, cardamom, and nutmeg, which have been folded into a betel-nut leaf secured with a clove.

Juniper Incense

This is based on a recipe of 1662.

2 tbsp juniper berries, well crushed
2 tsp gum benzoin powder
2 tsp frankincense powder
3 drops lemon oil
3 drops clove oil
3 drops rose oil

Mix all the ingredients together. To burn, light a disk of incense charcoal on a heatproof dish. Leave it until it is gray. Put about 1 teaspoon of the incense on the lighted disk.

Spiced oils and soaps have a warming and soothing effect. This range of spiced cosmetics contains cinnamon bark and leaf, ginger oil, mustard, lemongrass, and clove oil.

Winter Warmer

On a chilly day, this will warm you right through. It also helps to stave off colds, coughs, and influenza.

¼ tsp cayenne pepper
⅔ cup boiling water

Put the cayenne pepper into a mug. Pour in the boiling water. Cover and leave until the water has cooled just enough to drink comfortably.

SPICES IN COSMETICS AND PERFUMES

Living in fragrant surroundings and having a sweetly scented body have always enhanced a person's well-being, and through the ages spices have helped to bring this about.

Spices are important ingredients in potpourris and pomanders. Traditionally, they have also been burned or simmered over the fire to fumigate rooms, and crushed and put into small cheesecloth bags, known as sweet bags, to be placed in chests among clothes and linen. There have even been special spice mixtures to scent kid gloves.

Toilet waters, colognes, and vinegars have all been scented with spice. One of the most famous toilet waters was Carmelite Water, first made by nuns in the Abbey of St. Just in 1379 (see page 21). Honey Water was invented in the 17th century by George Wilson, apothecary to James II of England. Wilson said it "soothes the skin and gives one of the most agreeable scents that can be smelt." Spiced vinegars, made by steeping herbs and spices, such as cloves and cinnamon, in a good-quality wine vinegar, were used as scents and added to baths as skin softeners.

In modern perfumery, cinnamon and cassia, favorites with the ancient Greeks, are still used. Cardamom is favored in France and the United States. Caraway is mixed with lavender and bergamot in cheaper

preparations, and allspice is common in men's toiletries. Allspice, caraway, cinnamon, cassia, nutmeg, and even dill help to scent soaps, and allspice and nutmeg are popular in hair lotions.

Face preparations, too, can be made with spices. In the East, an infusion of coriander seeds serves as a complexion bleach. In India, a cosmetic face and body pack to clear the skin is based on turmeric, and in Asia turmeric water and a face powder containing turmeric are used to give a golden glow to the skin.

You can make your own perfumes from essential oils. Spice oils are usually mixed with

Chafing Dish

This is excellent for getting rid of kitchen or tobacco smells.

1 tsp cloves
Small piece cinnamon stick
1 sprig fresh marjoram or ½ tsp dried
1 tsp sugar
½ cup rosewater

Put all the ingredients into a small skillet. Set them on top of the stove and bring them to a boil. Simmer gently so the scent is released until the rosewater has almost all evaporated.

Essential oils, a base oil, and a small dish for blending are all that are needed to make a home aromatherapy kit.

light herbal or citrus oils to produce a full, rounded scent. Homemade perfumes have gentle background fragrances, rather than an assertive scent. To create a perfume, start with a base oil, such as jojoba or almond. Pour this into a dark glass bottle. Add the essential oils, drop by drop, cover, and shake. Label. Leave in a dark place for two weeks before using.

Lavender, oakmoss, and coriander perfume: 2 teaspoons jojoba or almond oil, 4 drops lavender oil, 3 drops oakmoss oil, 2 drops coriander oil.

Neroli, Sandalwood, and Coriander Perfume: 2 teaspoons jojoba or almond oil, 8 drops neroli oil, 8 drops sandalwood oil, 3 drops coriander oil.

Clary sage, mandarin, and juniper perfume: 2 teaspoons jojoba or almond oil, 4 drops clary sage oil, 4 drops mandarin oil, 3 drops juniper oil.

SPICE OILS FOR AROMATHERAPY

Aromatherapy is the use of essential oils for healing or for general well-being. Most of the spice oils have a warming and stimulating effect, in contrast to the refreshing and uplifting greener scents of herbs. Below is a list of the main spice oils and their different uses. Never apply them neat to your skin. Very small

Indigestion Remedy

Drink this after a large meal, or if indigestion strikes in the night. This recipe was popular with Victorian gentlemen.

½ tsp caraway seeds
2 cardamom seeds, removed from the pod
1 cup boiling water
honey to taste

Using a mortar and pestle, crush the caraway and cardamom seeds together. Put them into a jug. Pour in the boiling water. Cover and leave for 10 minutes. Strain into a mug. Add honey to taste and drink while it is warm.

This wooden box belonged to an Egyptian lady c.1800 B.C. *It contains a range of toilet articles and perfume bowls.*

amounts should be diluted in a carrier oil, such as almond or palm oil. Before treating yourself, you are advised to consult an aromatherapy directory or visit an aromatherapist.

Black pepper: A good digestive; stimulating for the circulation; combats colds and influenza; fights lethargy and mental fatigue; tones muscles; said to be an aphrodisiac.

Cardamom: A good digestive; combats exhaustion and mental fatigue; warming, stimulating and said to be an aphrodisiac.

Cinnamon: Use only in room vaporizers and never directly on your skin, because it can be an irritant. This oil is a good choice for fumigating a sick room. It is stimulating and also reputed to be an aphrodisiac.

Clove: Use only as a room scent and to fumigate the sick room, because it can irritate skin. Its fragrance is warming and stimulating.

Coriander: Digestive; good for aching muscles; stimulates circulation; fights colds and influenza; combats exhaustion and mental fatigue; warming.

Cumin: Use for its fragrance as a room scent only. It is useful for fumigating a sickroom and it will also stimulate a sluggish digestion.

Fennel seed: For flatulence and constipation; stimulates the appetite; helps heal bruises; aids in combating fluid retention and cellulite; eases chest infections; warming and stimulating.

Ginger: For arthritis, rheumatism, and muscular aches and pains; aids circulation; fights influenza, coughs, colds, and sore throats; helps travel sickness, nausea, and flatulence; combats exhaustion and mental fatigue; warming, stimulating, and said to be aphrodisiac.

Juniper: Helps rheumatism; combats acne, oily skin and eczema; fights colds and influenza; decreases cellulite; eases anxiety and nervous tension; calming; warming.

Vanilla: Often used purely for its scent; can be uplifting, pampering, and comforting; said to be an aphrodisiac.

𝒞innamon oil makes a stimulating room scent.

𝒢inger oil is warming and helps to combat exhaustion and mental fatigue.

Mustard Footbath

A mustard footbath will revive both your spirits and your aching feet. The Epsom salts make it very invigorating. If they are not available, use 2 tablespoons of sea salt plus 2 tablespoons baking soda. Have ready a large washing up bowl and a bath towel.

4 tbsp mustard powder
3 tbsp Epsom salts

Put the mustard powder and the Epsom salts into a bowl. Pour in enough hot water to cover your feet up to the ankles. Leave until it feels pleasantly warm.
Sit in a comfortable chair with your feet in the bowl and relax for 10 minutes. Dry your feet thoroughly and give them a massage with an aromatherapy oil or a special foot lotion.

Ginger and Lemon Soother

Drink this warming and comforting drink if you feel a cold developing. It is also very soothing for a cough.

4 thin slices fresh gingerroot, cut across the root
1 thick slice lemon
1 tsp honey or 1 tbsp concentrated apple juice
1 cup boiling water

Put the gingerroot, lemon slice, and honey or apple juice concentrate into a mug. Pour in the boiling water and stir well. Leave until it has cooled down enough to drink. Stir again, pressing on the lemon and ginger.

Carmelite Water

Use this as a body splash after a bath.

1¼ cups vodka
6 tbsp chopped angelica leaves and stems
6 tbsp chopped lemon balm leaves
1 tbsp coriander seeds, bruised
1 tbsp cloves, bruised
2 nutmegs, cut into chips

Put the vodka into a jar with the remaining ingredients. Cover tightly and shake. Leave in a warm place for three weeks, shaking every day. Strain and rebottle. It can be used straight away.

21

SPICES IN THE KITCHEN

SINCE EARLY TIMES ALL OVER THE WORLD, SPICES HAVE BEEN POUNDED AND MIXED TO IMPROVE THE FLAVOR AND SOMETIMES THE APPEARANCE OF FOOD AND DRINK. MEAT AND FISH, PUDDINGS AND DESSERTS, SAUCES AND PICKLES, BREAD AND CAKES HAVE ALL BENEFITED FROM THE SUBTLE—AND SOMETIMES NOT SO SUBTLE—ADDITION OF SPICES.

In the Indus valley, about 3000 B.C., food was seasoned with mustard, turmeric, and ginger. The remains of coriander seeds have been found in a Bronze Age settlement in Kent, England, and we know that hot peppers and vanilla were used by the Incas.

The Romans loved spices and recognized they both flavored food and stimulated digestion. Frequently mentioned in Roman recipes are coriander, cinnamon, cassia, and ginger, but the favorite was pepper, which was added to sweet and savory dishes. Roman sauces included quite complicated spice mixtures in large quantities. It might seem to us they were very strongly flavored, but no one knows just how much meat the sauces were intended for or how much flavor the spices might have retained after journeys lasting up to two years from their origins.

In India around A.D. 1, cardamom, coriander, cumin, and turmeric were being used to make *kari* (the origin of our word curry), either as a dry dish or as a liquid sauce to pour over rice. Although spicy, these were not the hot curries that are most familiar today, because fiery red peppers were unknown then.

The Celts who settled on the Atlantic coast of France favored cumin and used it with salt and vinegar to flavor baked fish. The Saxons in Britain had little access to most spices, although pepper was important to them, and spices were one of the rare luxuries allowed to monks during the Dark Ages.

In the medieval period, with the opening up of trade routes, the kitchens of the rich all over Europe welcomed cinnamon, ginger, saffron, and cardamom, plus the newly discovered nutmeg, mace, cloves, grains of paradise (a type of pepper), zedoary and galingale (both of the ginger family), and cubebs (peppery Javanese spice berries). They were so expensive, even for the most wealthy, that they were stored in special locked

A Bronze Age jar of the type probably used to keep a treasured supply of spices.

A 14th-century painting of an Indian spice market.

A Hunting Pudding

Beat eight eggs, and mix them with a pint of good cream, and a pound of flour, beat them well together, and put to them a pound of beef suet chopped very fine, a pound of currants well cleaned, half a pound of jar raisins stoned and chopped small, a quarter of a pound of powdered sugar, two ounces of candied citron, the same of candied orange cut small, grate a large nutmeg, and mix all well together, with half a gill of brandy, put it in a cloth, and tie it up close, it will take four hours boiling.

ELIZABETH RAFFALD, *THE EXPERIENCED ENGLISH HOUSEKEEPER*, 1732

22

In the 16th century, spices were used to improve the flavor of plain monastry food.

The kitchen of a 16th-century inn. Spices would have been stored in a locked cupboard, with small amounts being brought out only when needed.

Cayenne Vinegar,
or Essence of Cayenne

INGREDIENTS – *½ oz of cayenne pepper, ½ pint of strong spirit, or 1 pint of vinegar.*

Mode – *Put the vinegar, or spirit, into a bottle, with the above proportion of cayenne, and let it steep for a month, when strain off and bottle for use. This is excellent seasoning for soups or sauces, but must be used very sparingly.*

ISABELLA BEETON, *BEETON'S BOOK OF HOUSEHOLD MANAGEMENT*, 1861

cupboards and only released in essential amounts for the use of the cook. Medieval foods combined the sweet and the savory, and it was quite usual for meat and fruit to appear together in the same dish, their flavors blended with the aid of spice mixtures. Spices were frequently used as colorings for medieval dishes: cloves and sandalwood for red; saffron for yellow; and indigo for blue. Cinnamon was one of the best loved medieval spices, although mustard and pepper were usually all the poor could afford. Mustard was made into an accompanying sauce, as now, and was served with dishes such as boar's head and brawn.

In the 16th century freshly discovered spices traveled to Europe and elsewhere from the New World. Allspice was soon adopted to cure meats and for pickling and salting. Red chili peppers went to India to give heat to *karis*. They also became popular in western Europe

in the form of a clean-flavored condiment that was used during the 18th and 19th centuries at least as much as ordinary pepper.

Sweet and savory flavors gradually became more separate, and single spices began to be used as well as mixtures. In England, caraway became the favorite spice for cakes and fruit-based sweets. In Shakespeare's *Henry IV, Part 2*, Squire Shallow invites Falstaff to "a . . . pippin with a dish of caraways," and in 1629, John Parkinson, an English herbalist and gardener, remarked that "The seed is much used to be put among baked fruit, or into bread, cakes, etc., to give them a relish."

Pickles grew popular in the 17th century and, all over Europe, dill was added to pickled cucumbers. Nutmeg, mace, and ginger found their way into jars of pickled mushrooms. In England, turmeric from India was an essential ingredient in the newly discovered piccalilli, and ginger and red pepper were used in mango and marrow chutney.

Spice mixtures began to appear in cookbooks. A recipe of 1682 for mixed spice contained 1 ounce

Boar's head with mustard was popular Christmas fare in medieval and Tudor England. It survived even longer at Queen's College, Oxford, where the ceremony of "Bringing in the Boar's Head" is still observed.

23

A modern-day cowboy tending a cattle drive in Montana. It was on cattle drives in the 19th century that chili con carne was developed.

each of pepper, cinnamon, cloves, and nutmeg, with a further 1 pound pepper. Blends for salting and pickling meats included juniper, allspice, and cloves. By 1780 there were recipes for premixed curry powders.

In Britain in the 18th century, nutmeg flavored nearly every sweet dish and its outer coating, mace, was a favourite for potted meats and fish, and in stuffings for veal (a popular meat) and turkey. Due to British links with India, curries were popular, incorporating the old and the new, hotter spices. The 19th century, on both sides of the Atlantic, was the age of bottled sauces. These were made with a mixture of spices and sometimes a fruit or vegetable, such as tomato or mushroom. They were bottled and stored on the shelf until needed for adding to stews, pies, gravies, and broiled meats. Ice cream became popular in the late 19th century and the traditional spice for this was vanilla.

In the United States, hot red pepper, paprika, mustard, and black pepper were popular spices. Chili con carne (chili with meat) was devised just after the American Civil War. The Native Americans and chuck wagon cooks on cattle drives used ground chilies to preserve meats.

A Well-Spiced Pottage

A pottage was a thick soupy stew.

Take and sethe [boil] a few eyron [eggs] in red Wyne; then take and draw them throw a straynoure with a gode mylke of Almaundys [almonds]; then caste thereto Roysonys of Coraunce [raisins of Corinth], Dates y-taylid [taken from the stalk], grete Roysonys [large raisins], Pynes [pine nuts], pouder Pepir [ground pepper], Sawndrys [sandalwood], Clouys [cloves], Maces, hony y-now [enough], a lytil doucete [cheesecake], and Salt; then bynde hym uppe flat with a lytyl flowre of Rys [rice flour], and let him ben Red [colour it red] with Saunderys [sandalwood], and serve him in flatte; and if thou wolt, in fleyssh tyme [not Lent or a Friday, when meat was forbidden] caste vele y-choppid [chopped veal] ther-on, not to smale [small].

FROM THE *HARLEAN MANUSCRIPT*,
c. 1420

BUYING, STORING, AND USING SPICES

Today spices are flown and shipped all over the world soon after they have been picked and dried in their country of origin. When they reach the stores, they should be at the peak of their condition so their flavors are at full strength.

Spices should always be bought in small amounts because their flavor diminishes with age. If you already have storage jars for your spices, there is no need to keep buying them in glass containers, which tend to be more expensive.

PREPARING SPICES

Ground spices need no preparation. Whole spices can be used as they are for some recipes. For others they must be crushed or ground.

You can crush or grind your own spices, singly or in mixtures, to suit particular dishes. The best way to coarsely crush whole spices is by using a medium- to large-size mortar and pestle. Make sure the pestle fits snugly into the mortar and you find it comfortable to use. A heavy pestle is more efficient than a light-weight one.

To grind whole spices to a powder, dry-roast them first by putting them into a heavy skillet and moving them around over low heat for 10 minutes. Allow to cool, then grind them in a spice grinder or a small coffee grinder, preferably one devoted solely to the purpose. If you use your regular coffee grinder, you will need to wipe it thoroughly before and immediately afterward. Grind spices in amounts of 1 to 2 tablespoons. Nutmegs are large enough to be hand grated directly into a dish. Use a fine kitchen grater or a special nutmeg grater.

USING GROUND SPICES

Bread, cakes, cookies, and flour-based puddings: Add directly to the batter or dough.
Soups, stews, casseroles, and curries: If the preparation involves sautéing onions first, add the spices just before the onions are soft and stir them on the heat for a few minutes. Do not let them burn. For cold-start dishes, coat the meat and/or vegetables in the given amount of spice before putting them into the pan and adding water or stock.
Sauces: Add when sautéing as above; or if the sauce is thickened with flour, add with the flour as in a mustard sauce.
Salad dressings: Use in small quantities; let the dressing stand for 30 minutes before using.
Rice: Where oil is not used in the cooking technique, mix into the rice before adding the water. Where oil is used, mix the rice and spice into the oil over low heat before adding water.
Chutneys: Add at the beginning of cooking with the main ingredients.

USING WHOLE SPICES

Breads and cakes: Caraway, cumin, dill, and anise seeds are added whole to doughs and batters; nutmeg is grated into the batters; cardamom seeds are added crushed.
Stocks: Add spices whole with water; strain after cooking.
Spiced vinegars and pickles: Add whole before bringing vinegar to a boil; may or may not be tied in cheesecloth.
Pâtés and terrines: Add crushed to the mixture; grate in nutmeg.
Broiled meats and roasts: Coat meats in crushed spices—for example, steak au poivre; stick cloves into roast ham before putting it into the oven.
Stuffings: Add crushed to the mixture.
Desserts: Infuse whole spices in syrups or milk —for example, in poached fruit or milk puddings; grate nutmeg onto milk puddings and custards.

Spices should be stored in containers that protect them from air and light. Traditional storage drawers like these or dark-colored glass jars are ideal.

THE SPICE DIRECTORY

SPICES COME IN MANY FORMS AND FLAVORS, AND ARE DERIVED FROM DIFFERENT PARTS OF MANY HERBACEOUS AND FRUITING PLANTS, VINES, AND TREES: FLOWER BUDS, FRUITS, SEEDS, AND ROOTS—EVEN THE FRAIL FILAMENTS AT THE HEART OF A FLOWER.

ANETHUM GRAVEOLENS (*DILL*)

Dill is native to the Mediterranean regions and southern Russia, and it has become particularly important in eastern and northern Europe. Dill seed comes from an umbelliferous plant of which the leaves are also used. The seeds are sold and used whole. The chief culinary uses of dill seed are in flavoring pickles, particularly cucumber, and as an ingredient in bread, cakes, pies, and sauces. Medicinally, dill has been used for soothing babies and relieving wind.

BRASSICA ALBA, BRASSICA JUNCEA, BRASSICA NIGRA (*WHITE, BROWN, AND BLACK MUSTARD*)

Mustard is probably of Asiatic origin, although it was taken very early across Europe and beyond. The annual plant is now grown in most temperate countries. At one time, *Brassica nigra*, or black mustard, was the most popular, but it has been superseded by *B. juncea* (brown mustard), which is easier to harvest. Black and brown mustards have pungent flavors, whereas white mustard provides a sharp hotness. Most prepared mustard powders are a mixture of black or brown with a little white, plus wheat flour and turmeric. The seeds are also sold whole, mainly for pickling.

CAPSICUM ANNUUM (*PAPRIKA*)

Paprika is a ground spice, produced mainly in Eastern Europe and Spain and in California from the dried seed pods of a small, sweet, red pepper, which is grown as an annual. It is a dark, brown-red colored spice with a warm, pungent flavor but no hotness. In Hungary, paprika is the main flavoring for hearty meat dishes, such as *gulyas*; in Spain and Portugal it is used for fish and for spicy sausages; and it also features in Middle Eastern and Indian dishes. Paprika is rich in vitamin C and it is thought to stimulate the appetite and digestive juices.

CAPSICUM FRUTESCENS (*CHILI*)

Chilies can be bought whole, either fresh or dried, and also ground into an orange powder, which has a clean, very hot flavor. Chilies are native to Mexico and to Central and South America, but were taken to Europe in the 16th century. From there they spread quickly to the Middle East, India, and China. They are now grown by three-quarters of all the spice-producing countries. Chilies are an ingredient in curries and many other hot, spiced dishes, and the ground powder makes a clean-tasting component of fish dishes and sauces.

CARUM CARVI (*CARAWAY*)

Caraway seeds come from an umbelliferous plant native to Britain, northern Europe, Scandinavia, Canada, the United States, Asia, Siberia, and the Middle East. Most of the world's supplies now come from the Netherlands. The seeds are small, thin, brown and sweetly spiced. They are a frequent ingredient in bread and cakes and go well with many vegetables. They are added to apple pie and used to flavor wine, brandy, and liqueur.

CINNAMOMUM CASSIA (*CASSIA OR CINNAMON BARK*)

Cassia, or cinnamon bark, is a variety of cinnamon which has a stronger, more bitter flavor than *Cinnamomum zeylanicum* (below), and is the type of cinnamon most favored in the United States. The bark is available ground from some specialist shops.

CINNAMOMUM ZEYLANICUM (*CINNAMON*)

Cinnamon is native to Southeast Asia, India, and China and is now grown mainly in Sri Lanka, India, Indonesia, and Vietnam. It is a member of the laurel family and the part used is the fragrant bark which is sold both in rolled sticks and as a fine, dull brown powder.

CORIANDRUM SATIVUM (*CORIANDER*)

Coriander is native to southern Europe, North Africa and the Middle East, and the best quality still comes from these regions. It is also grown commercially in India and can be cultivated in warm herb gardens in temperate climates. Coriander is an annual, umbelliferous plant of which the leaves and the small, round seeds are used. Both have a rich, pungent flavor. The seeds are sold whole and ground. Whole, they are used for pickling; coarsely crushed, they are put into breads in several parts of the world. Ground coriander is a popular curry ingredient. It can also be added to cakes, spiced cookies and fruit pies.

CROCUS SATIVUS (*SAFFRON*)

Saffron is produced from the dried stigmas of a large purple crocus, and is believed to have originated from the area around Turkey, but since the Middle Ages, the best saffron has come from Spain. It is expensive because it takes 60,000 flowers to make 1 pound of saffron, and all the stigmas are picked out by hand before drying. Saffron is probably one of the world's oldest food colorings. In Spain, it is a key ingredient of paella, in France, bouillabaisse and in Italy, risotto. In Britain and the United States, it is used to make saffron cake.

CUMINUM CYMINUM (*CUMIN*)

Cumin is an umbelliferous plant which originated in the Nile Valley but has been grown since early times all around the Mediterranean and in India and China. It can be cultivated in herb gardens in temperate climates but it needs a very warm spot and a hot summer to be successful. Cumin seeds are small, thin and brown, with a dry, slightly bitter, spicy flavor. Whole and ground, cumin is used in curries and spiced dishes of meat, fish, and vegetables. The seeds are put into bread.

CURCUMA LONGA (*TURMERIC*)

Turmeric is related to ginger and is the dried root of a plant that came originally from Indonesia and China. It has been grown in India for thousands of years and has been called the Indian saffron, which is a pity, since it has its own flavor and color and should not be regarded as a substitute. In India, turmeric colors and flavors rice and a variety of curry dishes. It is also used in fruit drinks, cakes, jellies and confectionery. In the West it is mixed with mustard to serve as a food coloring.

27

ELETTARIA CARDAMOMUM (*CARDAMOM*)

Cardamom is the seed of a plant native to India and Southeast Asia. The seeds grow in small, hard pods, and remain in these when sold. They are usually removed from the pods before use and are sometimes gently roasted to bring out the flavor. Cardamom is also available ground. It has a pungent, sweet scent and flavor and is an important ingredient of spice mixtures known as *garam masala*. Cardamom flavors breads in Scandinavia, coffee in the Middle East, and many curry dishes.

EUGENIA CARYOPHYLLATA (*CLOVE*)

Cloves are native to the Molucca Islands, which are now part of Indonesia. Most cloves now come from Tanzania, although small amounts are exported from Sri Lanka, Indonesia, and Madagascar. The part used is the flower bud, picked when red and then dried. They are available whole and ground. Cloves have both sweet and savory uses. In the East, they are used in curries. In the West, they are stuck into a baked ham or a leg of lamb, and added to pickles and sauces. They also flavor fruit pies, cakes and confectionery.

ILLICIUM VERUM (*STAR ANISE*)

Star anise is a native of China. It is a tree with large shiny leaves and small yellow flowers that are followed by star-shaped fruits. When dried, these fruits are a deep red-brown with a flavor of spiced aniseed. Star anise is very strong and in China a single seed is used to flavor a whole baked fish or the meat dish called "red cooked pork."

JUNIPERUS COMMUNIS (*JUNIPER*)

Juniper berries are the small, round, blue-black fruits of an evergreen tree that is native to Britain and Europe, North America, North Africa, and Asia. They have a mild but oily and slightly pungent flavor and scent, and are usually added to preserved meats, game dishes and winter vegetables. They are also used to flavor gin.

MYRISTICA FRAGRANS (*NUTMEG AND MACE*)

The nutmeg tree, native to the Moluccas in Indonesia, provides two spices: nutmeg and mace. When the thick outer coating of the nut splits, inside is the small brown nutmeg enclosed in a cage of red mace, which, after drying, becomes deep yellow. Both mace and nutmeg have always had sweet and savory uses. Mace is most often employed in the West for flavoring meat dishes, particularly potted meats and sausages; and nutmeg is added to meatballs, potato dumplings, and dishes made with cheese or egg. Both are used in desserts, puddings, cakes, and mulled drinks.

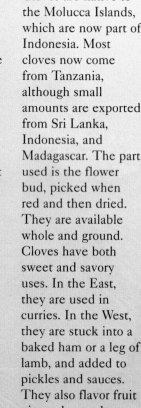
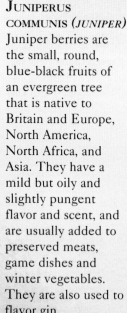

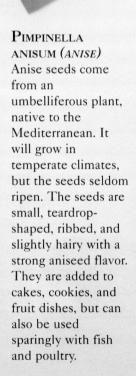

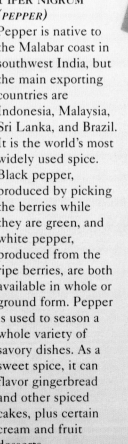

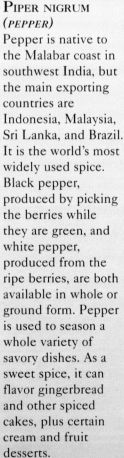

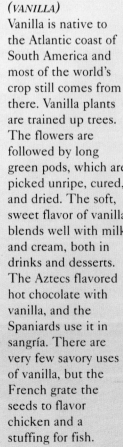

PIMENTA DIOICA (ALLSPICE)

Allspice trees are native to the Caribbean and most of the world's crop still comes from Jamaica. The small round berries vary in size and are dark gray-brown with a rough skin. They have a very delicate, bittersweet flavor and are mainly used for preserving meats and making sauces and ketchups. Ground allspice is put into puddings, cakes, cookies, gingerbread, and pumpkin pie.

PIMPINELLA ANISUM (ANISE)

Anise seeds come from an umbelliferous plant, native to the Mediterranean. It will grow in temperate climates, but the seeds seldom ripen. The seeds are small, teardrop-shaped, ribbed, and slightly hairy with a strong aniseed flavor. They are added to cakes, cookies, and fruit dishes, but can also be used sparingly with fish and poultry.

PIPER NIGRUM (PEPPER)

Pepper is native to the Malabar coast in southwest India, but the main exporting countries are Indonesia, Malaysia, Sri Lanka, and Brazil. It is the world's most widely used spice. Black pepper, produced by picking the berries while they are green, and white pepper, produced from the ripe berries, are both available in whole or ground form. Pepper is used to season a whole variety of savory dishes. As a sweet spice, it can flavor gingerbread and other spiced cakes, plus certain cream and fruit desserts.

VANILLA PLANIFOLIA (VANILLA)

Vanilla is native to the Atlantic coast of South America and most of the world's crop still comes from there. Vanilla plants are trained up trees. The flowers are followed by long green pods, which are picked unripe, cured, and dried. The soft, sweet flavor of vanilla blends well with milk and cream, both in drinks and desserts. The Aztecs flavored hot chocolate with vanilla, and the Spaniards use it in sangría. There are very few savory uses of vanilla, but the French grate the seeds to flavor chicken and a stuffing for fish.

ZINGIBER OFFICINALE (GINGER)

Marco Polo found ginger in China in the 13th century. By the 16th century it was growing in the American colonies, the West Indies, and India. The part used is the rhizome, or root, of a lily-like plant, which grows in warm, humid climates. Gingerroot can be bought fresh, and is usually grated for adding to curries and dishes with a Chinese flavor. Dried gingerroot, processed by scraping the skin from the roots before drying them, is hard and white, and is mainly used to flavor pickling vinegars and mulled drinks. Ground ginger is composed of this "white ginger," plus "black ginger" made by leaving the skin on the roots and scalding them before drying.

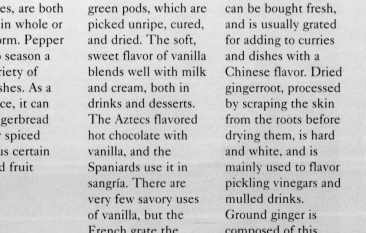

A WORLD OF SPICES

SPICES ARE GROWN IN ALL CONTINENTS. FROM MUSTARD SEEDS IN ENGLAND AND CANADA TO THE NUTMEG OF THE INDONESIAN ISLANDS, THEY ARE A VITAL PART OF WORLD TRADE AND CUISINE.

Red, hot, and spicy: chili peppers in an Indian market (far right).

Spices, herbs, and cooked foods create a colorful display on a marketstall in Bangkok, Thailand.

Listed below are just some of the countries and regions that grow and export spices.

THE UNITED STATES AND CANADA

The climate of North America varies considerably from north to south. The most northerly spice here is mustard seed which can be found in northern Canada about level with the tip of Greenland. Paprika is produced on a large scale in hotter California. The state cannot supply all of the United States' needs,

but alone provides more than any single country. During the hot, dry weather of summer and early fall the small red pods of *Capsicum annuum* are picked as they become ripe and fully mature. Unlike the practice in European countries, they are not cured or sun-dried, but are carried straight from the plant into hot-air tunnels or stainless steel belt driers. This produces a paprika that is sweet rather than pungent, enabling it to be used quite liberally in cooked and manufactured products for both its flavor and its deep red color.

The chili peppers produced in California tend to be milder than those grown farther south. They include varieties such as Ruby King and California Wonder, and are popular eaten raw, either in salads or as an accompaniment to cooked meats.

MEXICO AND CENTRAL AND SOUTH AMERICA

The home of the chili pepper is in Mexico and in Central and South America, where it has been grown for thousands of years. Colorful displays of chilies of all shapes and sizes can be seen in town markets and grocers' stores and being sold by farmers along country roadsides.

Some chilies are used fresh and others are dried. The cayenne, a long, thin chili that comes in a variety of sizes, is generally eaten fresh, and so is the guero, which is mild-flavored and light green. Chilies that are dried before use include the mirasol colorado, a large, dark red, mild variety from Peru; the tiny red

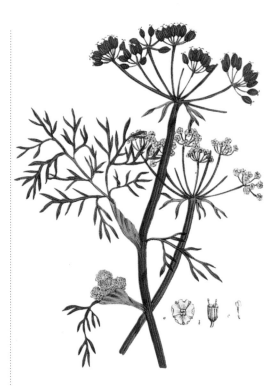

pequin; the mild ancho, which is the most popular Mexican red chili; and the mulato, which is large, dark, and very pungent.

The chili features prominently in Mexican cooking and almost every part of Mexico has its own variety. Mexicans are so used to eating chilies they commonly pick them straight from the plant and eat them raw. The Peruvian chili, called *aji*, is the main flavoring in the thick soups and stews that are eaten in Chilian homes. It can be found for sale in Indian markets.

Other spices grown in South America include allspice, picked from wild trees in Mexico, Guatemala, El Salvador, and Honduras; turmeric in Honduras and Peru; cardamom in Panama and southern Mexico; and nutmeg and mace in Guyana, French Guiana, and Honduras. Plantations in Brazil produce a light, white pepper known in the spice trade as Brazilian white pepper. It is grown along the Amazon river.

The explorer Christopher Columbus, who discovered chili peppers in the New World.

Pungent caraway seeds can be grown in the temperate climate of Holland and as far north as Scandinavia (far right).

THE CARIBBEAN

The Caribbean is home to the allspice tree. Its name derives from the fact that when it was first discovered, it was thought to smell like a mixture of nutmeg, cinnamon, and mace. Not unlike peppercorns in appearance, allspice is also known as Jamaica pepper. Locally,

Crocus sativus, the saffron crocus. In Spain its tiny stigmas are picked out by hand to produce the coveted spice.

however, it is called pimento. Allspice has not achieved as much popularity as the other spices, but it is an important seasoning in many Caribbean dishes, including the fish dish known as blaff. It is also the principal flavoring in Pimento Dram, a popular Jamaican liqueur.

Most Jamaican allspice is grown on cultivated trees. The berries are picked by hand just before they are fully ripe, and sun-dried on concrete patios for up to 10 days before going through a first cleaning process. They are then sent to the Government Pimento Clearing House, where they are cleaned for a second time before being packed into bags for export.

Ginger, nutmeg, cloves, cinnamon, and chili peppers are also grown in the Caribbean.

ENGLAND

England once grew its own saffron, caraway, juniper, and mustard. Now, however, mustard is its only commercial spice. Both white and brown mustard seeds are grown in open fields on the eastern side of the country. Over the years, plant breeders have produced a succession of improved strains, and two of the latest are Newton (brown) and Kirby (white), named after the Norfolk parishes in which they were developed. The seed is sown between mid-March and early April, and the yellow flowers bloom throughout June as the crop grows to about 6 feet tall. Mechanical

31

The saffron festival in Spain celebrates the harvest of this much-loved plant.

harvesting takes place in August and September. The seeds are graded and cleaned and then stored in concrete silos of over 9,000-ton capacity. Both white and brown mustard seeds make a yellow powder when ground.

Brown mustard gives pungency and white provides hotness. Combined after milling, they make the ideal mustard powder. After pepper and salt, mustard is probably the most used spice in England. Mixed with water and other ingredients it has accompanied cold meats since medieval times. It is also added dry to white sauces, savory baked goods, and meat dishes.

THE NETHERLANDS

Together with Scandinavia, the Netherlands has always been a leading producer of caraway seeds. It now provides more than any other country in the world.

Caraway plants take two seasons to produce seeds. Round clusters of white flowers appear in May and the seeds are ready to harvest two months later. Harvesting begins when the oldest fruits have turned brown. If it was left any longer, the ripest seed heads would shatter and be lost. As an additional precaution, harvesting of the seed-bearing stems is done early in the morning while the dew is still on the plants, when the seeds fall less readily. The stems are stacked in piles and left for at least 10 days to dry and finish ripening. Then the seeds are threshed and cleaned and the stems fed to cattle.

A 16th-century Turkish manuscript showing merchants and spice traders measuring out and selling their goods.

SPAIN

Chili peppers, paprika, and saffron are Spain's chief spices. Spanish saffron is the finest in the world. It is grown on small family plots on the barren plains of La Mancha in south-central Spain. The saffron plant is a variety of crocus but, unlike most flowering crocuses, it is planted in July for harvesting in September. The plant has low, grasslike leaves, a pinkish stem, and a large, purple, lily-shaped flower. In the center of the flower are three orange-red stigmas. These constitute the saffron. The only way to harvest saffron is by hand. The flowers are cut, gathered up, and taken back to the farmhouse, where members of the family sit and pick out the stigmas and a small part of the style. These are dried in a kiln between layers of thick paper and then pressed to form small cakes. Saffron is expensive, but a little goes a long way, adding rich flavor and a soft yellow color.

EASTERN EUROPE

Paprika and coriander are the most familiar spices of Eastern Europe. Hungarian paprika is said to be the best, with the warmest, most pungent flavor and a light red color. Paprika (*Capsicum annuum*) was taken to Hungary in 1699 by the Turks, who had acquired it from South America by way of Spain and North Africa. In Magyar countries, paprika became the most used spice and a part of almost every celebratory dish.

The paprika harvest extends through the summer months. Locally, some of the pods are eaten fresh, while they are still yellow. Some people like to cut them in strips and dip them in salt. Most, however, are left until they are red and are cured for up to 25 days either by hanging the pods in long strands or by piling them up in a warm place. They are then dried in the sun for 15 days. Although generally not available separately, there are six different types of Hungarian paprika: "without bite"; "sweet"; "half-sweet"; "pink"; "strong"; and "special". The spice that we buy is usually a blend of several of these.

An old Hungarian proverb goes: "One man may yearn for fame, another for wealth, but everyone yearns for paprika goulash." Goulash, or *gulyas*, as it is known in Hungary, goes back to the 9th century and is the country's national dish. It originated with the Magyar shepherds, who stewed meat and onions gently over an open fire and carried them stored in a sheep's stomach, as provisions for when they were far from home with their grazing flocks. Paprika was added to the ingredients in the 18th century. Other traditional dishes that use paprika include *porkolt*, similar to *gulyas* but with more onions; *paprikas*, usually made with veal or chicken; and *tokany*, a more sophisticated and rich dish made with cream, goose liver, and vegetables.

INDIA

Large and colorful, with many culinary traditions, India is one of the world's foremost spice-producing countries. The significance of spices was recognized in India 3,000 years ago, when they were listed in Ayurvedic (Hindu medicine) writings. Today you will find them, both fresh and dried, piled in picturesque heaps in markets, such as the Crawford Market in Bombay. Two million of India's agricultural acres are devoted to the production of spices, of which the most important crops are chilies, pepper, turmeric, and ginger. Turmeric is cultivated in plantations about 3,500 feet above sea level, in areas with a hot, moist climate and well-drained soil. The plants are grown from rhizomes, called "fingers," which are harvested after about 10 months. They are boiled, cleaned, dried in the sun for about 10 days, and then polished. Turmeric is ground in spice mills, where everything—including the workers—is covered with a fine layer of yellow powder. A large percentage of India's turmeric is used in Indian homes, to flavor curries and color rice, and also as a dye, a cosmetic, a paint coloring, and an ingredient in medicines.

THE MOLUCCA ISLANDS

The Spice Islands, north of Australia and south of China, are the source of cloves, nutmeg, mace, pepper, and cassia. These tropical islands were the scene of much exploration, hardship, and fighting. Spice trees have always been much loved and revered by the Moluccan people, and none more so than the clove tree. Clove trees, by tradition, can only be planted in

the dark of the moon. The flower buds, which will become the cloves, grow in clusters on the ends of twigs, pale green at first and ripening to dark red. They are never allowed to open, because if they did they would lose their fragrance. Women and children pick complete twigs from the lower branches and the men pick from the upper ones, pulling them down with hooked poles. The buds are later picked off by hand and then dried in the sun for three days. It is possible to harvest two crops a year from a clove tree, but only one is taken, to avoid damage to the tree.

Nutmegs from the Spice Islands have long been popular in Europe. Here, a 15th-century French merchant carefully weighs them out for sale.

Spices make eye-catching displays in an Indian market.

33

CHAPTER ONE

APPETIZERS, SOUPS, AND SALADS

A spicy start to a meal can wake up your taste buds and stimulate your appetite, and a spice-flavored salad provides a refreshing contrast to rich food. The spices can be used dried or fresh to supply variations in texture and flavor.

APPETIZERS, SOUPS, AND SALADS

Spice combinations from all over the world give a wealth of flavor to warming soups, light appetizers and unusual salads. Mulligatawny Soup, Gujarati-style Carrot Salad, Indian Fruit Salad, *and* Onion Bhajis *are full of the flavors and aromas of the Indian subcontinent.*

From Southeast Asia come the creamy Thai-style Chicken and Coconut Soup *and small, spicy pieces of pork with peanut sauce, called* Pork Satay. Sesame Shrimp Toasts *evoke oriental flavors, and Europe*

gives us rich, red Borscht, *a soup made with beets and flavored with peppercorns and allspice.*

A hearty Peppered Farmhouse Pâté *is based on the classic French* pâté de campagne. *It has a delicious pungency from the combination of spices used: pickled pink and green peppercorns, juniper berries, mace, and black pepper. From the Middle East come* Lamb Böreks, *tiny pasties filled with ground lamb spiced with cinnamon.*

Still life, *P. Claesz*, c.*1630*.

INDIAN FRUIT SALAD

This is a delicious combination of salad, vegetables, mango and banana, tossed in a light dressing seasoned with cumin, cardamom, and mint. The salad benefits from marinating, so the flavor of the spices is released. Serve this dish as a refreshing appetizer to a rich Indian meal or as a delicate salad to accompany more strongly flavoured dishes, such as tandoori or dry curries.

SERVES 4

	DRESSING
1 pound peeled cooked potatoes	4 tbsp vegetable oil
1 cucumber	1 tbsp lime juice
4 tomatoes	6 cardamom pods
1 red onion	2 tsp cumin seeds
1 mango	2 tbsp chopped fresh mint
2 bananas	Salt and freshly ground black
Grated lime peel and mint	pepper
sprigs, to garnish	

First prepare the vegetables and fruit. Cut the potatoes into ¾-inch pieces; put them in a serving bowl. Cut the cucumber in half lengthwise and then in half again. Cut into ½-inch pieces. Quarter the tomatoes and remove the seeds. Chop the flesh. Thinly slice the onion. Mix all these vegetables into the potato. Peel the mango and slice the flesh off the large, flat seed in the center. Cut the flesh into cubes. Peel the bananas, then slice diagonally and mix into the vegetables.

For the dressing, put the oil and lime juice in a small bowl. Crack the cardamom pods and extract the small black seeds. Put them in a mortar and pestle, with the cumin seeds, and crush them. Mix into the oil and lime juice, add the mint, and season with salt and pepper.

Stir the dressing into the vegetables and fruit. Cover and chill for 2 hours. Allow to stand at room temperature for 30 minutes.

Serve garnished with lime peel and mint.

GUJARATI-STYLE CARROT SALAD

The region of Gujarat lies in the north of India. The Gujaratis have perfected the art of vegetarian cooking and use subtle spices to enhance staple ingredients. The flavors of Gujarat are echoed in this light salad: fresh gingerroot, mustard seeds, chili powder, and turmeric. The heat is mild, yet the flavor is full. This salad makes a perfect first course or accompaniment.

SERVES 4

	DRESSING
4 carrots	4 tbsp sunflower oil
1-inch piece of fresh gingerroot	1 tbsp lemon juice
1 red bell pepper	2 tsp lightly ground mustard
1 yellow bell pepper	seeds
6 ounces fresh pineapple flesh	½ tsp chili powder
2 tbsp sesame seeds	¼ tsp ground turmeric
Poppadoms, to serve	½ tsp salt

First prepare the salad ingredients. Peel the carrots and gingerroot and then slice into thin strips. Put in a mixing bowl. Halve and seed the peppers, cut in thin strips, and add to the bowl. Slice the pineapple flesh into small pieces and mix into the vegetables.

Put all the ingredients for the dressing in a small screw-topped jar. Seal and shake well to mix. Pour over the salad ingredients and mix well. Cover and chill for 2 hours. Leave the salad to stand at room temperature for 30 minutes before serving. Sprinkle each portion with a few sesame seeds and serve with poppadoms.

BORSCHT

There are many recipes for this classic Russian beet soup, but the flavoring derives from the sweet-sour piquant spices used, such as peppercorns and allspice berries. For perfect beet soup, you must use fresh beets and cook them from raw; this produces the best flavor and color. Vacuum-packed, cooked beets are a poor substitute because the flavor is watery; never use pickled varieties because the vinegar flavor will dominate.

SERVES 4

1 pound raw beets, peeled and cut into thin strips
1 tbsp white-wine vinegar
4 tbsp butter
5 cups vegetable stock
2 onions, finely chopped
2 carrots, peeled and cut into thin strips
2 potatoes, peeled and diced
2 garlic cloves, finely chopped

1 small white cabbage, finely shredded
6 black peppercorns
6 allspice berries
2 tsp sugar
1 tsp salt

TO SERVE
⅔ cup sour cream
4 tsp caraway seeds
2 tbsp chopped fresh parsley

Sprinkle the beets with the vinegar. Melt half the butter in a saucepan and gently fry the beets, stirring, for 3 to 4 minutes. Pour in half the stock and bring to a boil. Cover and leave to simmer for an hour, until tender.

Meanwhile, melt the remaining butter in another saucepan and gently fry the onions, carrots, potatoes, and garlic for 3 to 4 minutes. Pour in the remaining stock and bring to a boil. Cover and simmer for 20 minutes.

Add the cabbage, replace the lid, and leave to simmer for 10 minutes longer.

Crush the peppercorns and allspice berries in a mortar and pestle and add to the vegetables, with the cooked beet mixture. Add sugar and salt to taste: it should have a sharp taste. Serve with spoonfuls of sour cream and a sprinkling of caraway seeds and chopped parsley.

THAI-STYLE CHICKEN *and* COCONUT SOUP

This creamy soup is a popular light meal in Thailand. The blend of spices combines heat from red chilies and fragrance from galangal and lemongrass. The seasoning is a fish sauce (*nam pla*), a popular addition to Thai recipes. It is available from oriental stores.

SERVES 4

4 cups chicken stock
1¼ cups canned coconut milk
2 lemongrass stalks
1 lime
1 tbsp light soy sauce
1 tsp ground galangal
1 tsp ground coriander
2 small fresh red chilies, seeded and finely chopped

2 cups cooked, skinned chicken breast cut in thin strips
4 scallions, finely shredded
4 tbsp chopped fresh cilantro
*2 tbsp fish sauce (*nam pla*)*

Pour the stock and coconut milk into a saucepan. Slice the base off each stalk of lemongrass and discard any damaged leaves. Bend in half to "bruise" it and release the flavor. Add it to the saucepan. Pare the peel from the lime, keeping it in large pieces. Add it, along with the juice, soy sauce, galangal, ground coriander, and chilies. Bring gently to a boil. Add the chicken and leave to simmer for 10 minutes.

Discard the lemongrass and lime peel. Stir in the scallions, half the chopped cilantro, and the fish sauce. Ladle into warmed soup bowls. Serve sprinkled with the remaining cilantro.

41

SPICED OILS AND VINEGARS

SPICED RASPBERRY VINEGAR

A perfect vinegar for light salad dressings. It is subtly flavored with cinnamon, allspice, and black pepper.

MAKES ABOUT 2½ CUPS

8 ounces raspberries
1 cinnamon stick
1 tbsp allspice berries

2 tsp black peppercorns
2½ cups white-wine vinegar, chilled

Lightly crush the raspberries and put them in a clean, screw-topped jar. Break the cinnamon stick, lightly crush the allspice berries and peppercorns, and add to the raspberries. Pour the vinegar over. Seal and leave for at least 3 days, stirring several times each day to extract the maximum juice from the fruit. Strain through a fine strainer or cheesecloth and pour into sterilized bottles. Seal and label. Store in the refrigerator and keep for up to a month.

PROVENÇAL OLIVE OIL

A delicious oil for a salad dressing. Use a mild-flavored oil to allow the flavors of the herbs, peppercorns, and coriander and fennel seeds to develop.

MAKES 2 CUPS

1 large sprig each of fresh thyme, bay, and rosemary
1 tbsp black peppercorns
1 tbsp coriander seeds, lightly crushed

1 tbsp fennel seeds
1 garlic clove, peeled
2 cups light olive oil

Pack the herbs, peppercorns, seeds, and garlic in a clean, clear jar. Pour the olive oil over. Cover with a clean cloth and put in a warm place to steep for 2 weeks, stirring daily. Check for flavor, and strain, if preferred. Bottle and label.

42

MIDDLE EASTERN SPICED OIL

This makes a wonderful marinade for lamb or can be used to baste meat on the barbecue. Dried chilies make it hot and such spices as cinnamon, saffron, cumin, and coriander give it sweetness.

MAKES 2 CUPS

4 dried red chilies, split open
2 garlic cloves
1 large pinch of saffron
1 cinnamon stick, broken
1 tbsp cumin seeds, lightly crushed
1 tbsp coriander seeds, lightly crushed
2 strips pared lemon peel
2 cups light olive oil

Pack the chilies, garlic, spices, seeds, and lemon peel into a clean, clear jar. Pour in the olive oil, cover with a clean cloth, and leave to steep in a warm place, stirring every day. Check for flavor and strain, if preferred. Bottle and label.

SPICED GARLIC VINEGAR

Any vinegar can be used in this infusion but sherry vinegar is particularly good for oriental cookery. This vinegar is powerful in flavor and is enhanced by the pungency of the cloves and garlic.

MAKES ABOUT 2½ CUPS

1 bulb of garlic
1 tsp cloves, crushed
2½ cups sherry vinegar

Separate and peel the garlic cloves. For a very strong flavor, crush or chop the garlic; for a milder flavour, leave them whole. Put in a clean, screw-topped jar with the cloves and pour the vinegar over. Seal and leave in a cool, dark place. Taste after a week for flavor; then strain. Bottle and label. Store in a cupboard for up to 3 months.

SPICED LEMON VINEGAR

Use this vinegar as a marinade ingredient; it is particularly good with fish and poultry. It is mild in flavor and combines the woody flavors of allspice, mustard, peppercorns, mace, and cloves, with the fragrance of fresh lemon.

MAKES ABOUT 2½ CUPS

2½ cups white-wine vinegar
1 tbsp allspice berries
1 tbsp white mustard seeds
1 tbsp black peppercorns
1 mace blade
4 cloves
1 lemon, quartered
1 tbsp sea salt

Pour the vinegar into a saucepan and add the spices. Heat slowly and bring to a boil. Rub the lemon with the salt, put in a heatproof jar or bowl and pour the boiling spiced vinegar over. Cover with a cloth and leave to stand for 4 days. Strain, squeezing the juice from the lemon. Bottle and label. Store in the refrigerator for up to a month.

43

MULLIGATAWNY SOUP

This much-loved soup was invented in Madras many years ago; its name means "pepper water" in Tamil. This version, however, is not as fiery as the name suggests. It contains a wealth of comforting spices, such as gingerroot, cinnamon, cloves, and green chili, which combine to give a well-rounded flavor. It makes a warming meal on a cold day to serve accompanied by Indian naan bread.

SERVES 4

1 cup red lentils	5 cloves
5 cups vegetable stock	2 tsp ground coriander
2 tbsp vegetable oil	1 tsp ground turmeric
1 large onion, finely chopped	5 dried curry leaves, chopped
4 garlic cloves, finely chopped	⅔ cup canned coconut milk
1-inch piece of fresh gingerroot, finely chopped	Juice of ½ lemon
	1 tsp salt
1 fresh green chili, seeded and finely chopped	2 tbsp chopped fresh cilantro
	Naan bread, to serve
1 cinnamon stick	

Rinse the lentils in cold water. Then put them in a saucepan. Add the stock and bring to a boil. Simmer gently for 15 minutes, or until soft and pulpy.

Heat the oil and gently fry the onion, garlic, ginger, and chili for 3 to 4 minutes, until soft. Add all the spices and curry leaves, and fry, stirring, for 2 minutes, until the oil separates from the spices.

Stir the spice mixture, coconut milk, lemon juice, and salt into the cooked lentils. Heat through gently for 2 minutes. Discard the cinnamon and cloves. Serve sprinkled with chopped cilantro and accompanied by naan bread.

PEPPERED FARMHOUSE PÂTÉ

This recipe is based on the classic French *pâté de campagne*. The pâté has a delicious pungency from the spices used: pickled pink and green peppercorns, juniper berries, mace, and black pepper. Once baked, pressed, and chilled, the pâté is best served after standing at room temperature for 30 minutes for maximum flavor.

SERVES 6

8 ounces unsmoked bacon slices	1 tsp green peppercorns in brine, drained and rinsed
8 ounces salt pork, de-rinded and chopped	6 juniper berries, crushed
8 ounces chicken livers	½ tsp ground mace
8 ounces pig's liver, tubes removed, washed, and chopped	⅓ cup unsalted, shelled pistachio nuts
1 pound boneless, skinless chicken breast halves	1½ tsp salt
	Freshly ground black pepper
2 shallots, chopped	7 tbsp dry white wine
2 medium eggs, beaten	2 tbsp brandy
2 garlic cloves, crushed	4 bay leaves
1 cup fresh white bread crumbs	Toast, crusty French bread, or a salad, to serve
1 tsp pink peppercorns in brine, drained and rinsed	

Stretch each bacon slice with the back of a knife. Lay the bacon, overlapping, in a 3-pound terrine or loaf pan, to line the bottom and sides. Chill until required.

Put the salt pork, chicken and pig's livers, chicken, shallots, eggs, and garlic in a food processor and blend for 20 to 30 seconds, until well mixed. Pour into a mixing bowl and beat in the bread crumbs, peppercorns, juniper, mace, nuts, salt, and pepper. Stir in the wine and brandy. Cover and chill for an hour, to allow the flavors to develop.

Heat the oven to 350°F. Spoon the mixture into the bacon-lined terrine and lay the bay leaves on the top. Stand the terrine in a large roasting pan and pour in sufficient water to come 1 inch up the side of the terrine. Bake for 1½ to 1¼ hours, or until a skewer inserted in the middle comes out clean and hot and any juices that run out are clear.

Stand the terrine on a wire rack and leave to cool for an hour. Cover the top with waxed paper and lay weights on the top. Leave to chill overnight.

Remove the pâté from the terrine. Discard the bay leaves. Serve sliced with toasted bread, crusty French bread, or a salad.

Pepper

PEPPER (PIPER NIGRUM) HAS ALWAYS BEEN THE WORLD'S MOST IMPORTANT SPICE. IN INDIA IT IS CALLED THE "KING OF SPICES" AND IN OTHER COUNTRIES THE "MASTER SPICE." REFERENCES TO PEPPER APPEAR IN 3,000-YEAR-OLD SANSKRIT MEDICAL LITERATURE. IT WAS ONE OF THE EARLIEST ARTICLES OF COMMERCE, AND HAS ALWAYS BEEN AVAILABLE TO BOTH RICH AND POOR.

The origins of *Piper nigrum* lie in the damp jungles of the Malabar coast in southwestern India, but it is now widely cultivated in tropical areas of both the northern and southern hemispheres. The main exporting countries of today are Indonesia, Malaysia, Sri Lanka, and Brazil. Although pepper is mostly grown on small plots of land, the annual world exports amount to just over 25 percent of the total exports of all spices.

Pepper is a vine plant that climbs up jungle trees, and the berries grow in long clusters. A pepper vine takes three years to bear fruit but does not become fully mature until the ninth growing year. Each mature vine yields 4 to 5 pounds of dried berries. At harvest time, the pickers use ladders made from thick bamboo poles with steps on each side. The berries are picked by hand from the stems. Some are sun-dried on bamboo mats and others are kiln-dried. To produce black pepper, the berries are picked while still green, and dried until they become black and hard. This gives a strongly aromatic flavor in addition to being hot. For white pepper, the berries are picked when they have ripened and turned red. Before drying, they are stacked to make them ferment and the skins are then washed off. White pepper has a hot, clean flavor.

Green, red, and pink peppercorns are also available. Green peppercorns were first produced in 1971. They are picked unripe and dried artificially to fix the green color and yield a fresher flavor. They can also be left on the stems and pickled. Red peppercorns are usually found only in

46

White pepper has a hot, clean flavor. To produce white pepper, the berries are picked when they have ripened and turned red.

A 15th-century French manuscript showing pepper gatherers in Quilon, southwest India. Quilon is the oldest city on the Malabar coast and is still an important market for pepper.

pepper mixtures. They are not a true pepper, but the berries of a tropical bush.

The world-wide popularity of pepper in the kitchen stems from the fact that it is able to enhance the flavor of almost every type of food. It is often used during the preparation process, but also later to correct the seasoning of a dish, and finally at the table, at the diner's discretion.

BUYING PEPPER

Pepper can be bought whole or ground, singly or in mixtures of colors. Because the flavor deteriorates quickly once pepper is ground, it is best to buy whole peppercorns, keep them in a peppermill, and grind up the required amount when you need it. Keep separate mills for black and white peppers. For general flavoring, you may find that a mixture of two-thirds black and one-third white pepper suits all your requirements. This was originally used in France, where it was called *mignonette* pepper. This combination of peppercorns is available commercially, as are various "gourmet" combinations of black, white, green, and red.

Pepper

It [pepper] is generally employed as a condiment; but it should never be forgotten, that, even in small quantities, it produces detrimental effects on inflammatory constitutions.

ISABELLA BEETON, *BEETON'S BOOK OF HOUSEHOLD MANAGEMENT*, 1861

CULINARY USES

Black pepper: Add whole black peppercorns to stock, court bouillon, and boiled meats, and infuse them in milk before making a white sauce. Remove them before stirring the milk into the roux. Coarsely crushed, they find their place in brines and dry spicing mixtures, and can be pressed into meats before broiling or roasting. Put them in spiced breads, such as Indian naan. Use freshly milled black pepper in casseroles and stews, vegetarian dishes, pasta, and sweet spiced cakes.

White pepper: Many cooks like to use white pepper where the color of the finished dish is pale. It complements most vegetables, creamy soups, fish, dressings, and light-colored sauces.

Green peppercorns: These are generally used to make a sauce for poultry or game. They are also crushed and pressed into steak to make *steak au poivre.* Pickled green peppercorns can be mashed to a paste and mixed into sauces and savory butters.

MEDICINAL USES

Pepper has long been renowned as a digestive, to stimulate the appetite, and aid the digestion of rich foods.

Neat rows of pepper trees near Kuching in Sarawak, Borneo.

ONION BHAJIS

Homemade *bhajis* are quite different from those you may have bought; the secret is to make them small, so they cook right through and the batter is light and crisp. They shouldn't be too hot in flavor: use mild green chilies, cumin, and turmeric for the seasoning. It is well worth the effort of making your own and they make an excellent appetizer or canapé, served with a bowl of mango chutney.

SERVES 4

1½ cups (chick-pea) flour (from oriental stores)
1 tbsp sesame seeds
2 green chilies, seeded and finely chopped
1 tsp ground cumin
½ tsp ground turmeric
1 tsp salt
2 large onions, finely sliced

1 tbsp chopped fresh cilantro
¾ cup plus 2 tbsp water
Vegetable oil for deep-frying

To serve
Chopped fresh cilantro
Mango Chutney (see page 61)

Sift the flour into a bowl and mix in all the other ingredients, except the water. Gradually blend in the water, mixing thoroughly, until a thick batter is formed and the onions are well coated.

Heat the oil for deep-frying to a temperature of 350°F, or until a cube of day-old bread browns in 30 seconds. Drop heaped teaspoons of the onion batter into the oil, frying a few at a time, for 3 to 4 minutes or until golden brown. Don't make the *bhajis* too big or they won't cook in the middle. Drain on paper towels. Serve warm, garnished with chopped cilantro and accompanied by a bowl of mango chutney.

PORK SATAYS *with* SPICY PEANUT SAUCE

These spicy marinated Indonesian pork skewers, flavored with garlic, ginger, and five-spice powder, are accompanied by a rich coconut and peanut sauce.

SERVES 6

*1½ pounds lean pork
  tenderloin, trimmed*
*Lime wedges and green salad,
  to serve*

MARINADE
1 shallot, finely chopped
*1-inch piece of fresh ginger,
  finely chopped*
2 garlic cloves, finely chopped
Juice of 1 lime
1 tbsp five-spice powder
1 tbsp honey
4 tbsp light soy sauce
1 tbsp sesame seeds

PEANUT SAUCE
1¼ cups canned coconut milk
4 tbsp crunchy peanut butter
1 tbsp honey
1 tsp sesame oil
2 garlic cloves, crushed
1 tsp ground coriander
1 tsp ground cumin
½ tsp chili powder
2 tbsp dark soy sauce

Soak twelve 10-inch bamboo skewers in cold water for 30 minutes; this will prevent the meat from sticking to the skewers. Slice the pork into ¼-inch thick shreds and put in a shallow dish. Mix the marinade ingredients together and stir into the pork. Cover and chill for 2 hours.

Meanwhile, make the sauce. In a bowl, blend together the coconut milk, peanut butter, and honey; set aside. Heat the sesame oil gently and fry the garlic for a minute over low heat, to soften. Stir in the spices, soy sauce, and peanut mixture. Mix well and bring to a boil. Reduce the heat and simmer, stirring, for 5 minutes until thickened.

Heat the broiler to hot. Drain the pork shreds, reserving the marinade. Thread the pork onto the skewers in "S" shapes, to within 1 inch of the end. Cover the ends of the skewers with foil, to prevent their burning. Broil for 4 to 5 minutes on each side, brushing the pork with the reserved marinade to prevent its drying out, until cooked through. Discard the foil. Reheat the sauce if necessary. Serve the pork skewers with wedges of lime to squeeze over and a crisp green salad.

Lambswool

Lambswool is the hot, spiced ale that was once put into the wassail bowl at Christmas in England. The word wassail comes from the Saxon wase hael, *which means "be whole" or "be healthy," and was used to describe a form of Saxon toast, spoken before drinking to bring good fortune to the host and household. The custom of wassailing persisted in English country districts for many centuries. A special bowl full of hot, spiced beer or cider was taken to all the houses in the village or carried around the farm to bring good luck to the crops and the animals. To make lambswool, a good, strong beer was gently heated with spices, such as cinnamon and nutmeg. Then a stronger drink, such as sherry, brandy, or a powerful homebrew, was warmed and added. After the drink had been poured into the bowl, baked apples were floated on top. These dissolved into the drink to give it a "fluffy" appearance—hence the name lambswool.*

Wisselton, wasselton, who lives here?
We've come ter taste yer Christmas beer.
Up the kitchen and down the hall,
A peck of apples will serve us all.

SESAME SHRIMP TOASTS

These popular, crisp shrimp toasts make a tasty first course for a Chinese-style meal. They are delicately flavored with ginger and five-spice powder. Make sure the oil is at the correct temperature before you fry the shrimp mixture, or the toasts will be greasy.

SERVES 6

*8 ounces shelled uncooked
  shrimp, thawed if frozen
1 small egg yolk
4 scallions, finely chopped
½-inch piece of fresh ginger,
  peeled and finely chopped
1 tsp five-spice powder
2 tsp light soy sauce
1 tsp sesame oil*

*Salt
8 thin slices of white bread,
  crusts removed
2 tbsp sesame seeds
Oil for deep-frying
2 tbsp snipped fresh chives
Chopped scallion and red chili,
  to garnish*

Grind the shrimp into a paste in a food processor and mix with the egg yolk, scallions, ginger, five-spice, soy sauce, sesame oil, and a pinch of salt.

Cut each slice of bread into three equal fingers and spread the shrimp mixture on the fingers. Sprinkle with sesame seeds.

Heat the oil to 350°F. To judge the temperature without an oil thermometer, if a cube of day-old bread browns in the oil in 30 seconds, the oil is hot enough. Deep-fry a few shrimp toasts at a time, paste-side down for 1 to 2 minutes. Turn over and fry for 1 to 2 minutes longer, or until golden. Drain on paper towels. Sprinkle with chives, garnish with scallions and red chili tassels, and serve warm.

LAMB BÖREKS

In Turkey, you can find many varieties of these pastries, made with different fillings and flavored with a whole host of spices. This version is flavored with the sweeter spices, such as cinnamon and ground coriander, to complement the rich lamb and fruit filling. They make an excellent appetizer or light meal.

MAKES 16

FILLING
8 ounces lean ground lamb
1 small red onion, finely chopped
1 tbsp lemon juice
1 garlic clove, finely chopped
⅓ cup golden raisins
1 tsp ground cinnamon
1 tsp ground coriander
½ tsp cayenne pepper
2 tbsp chopped fresh cilantro
½ tsp salt

PASTRY
1 stick butter
1 tbsp olive oil
2 small eggs, beaten
⅔ cup plain yogurt
2 cups all-purpose flour
¼ tsp baking soda
1 tsp salt

TO SERVE
Lemon wedges and a crisp salad

Heat the oven to 400°F. Prepare the filling by mixing all the ingredients together. Cover and chill until required.

To make the pastry, melt the butter; set aside. Mix together the oil, half the beaten egg, and the yogurt. Sift the flour, baking soda, and salt into a bowl. Gradually mix in the melted butter and the yogurt mixture, to form a soft dough. Flour your hands, turn the dough onto a floured surface, and knead it for a few minutes, until smooth.

Roll out the dough thinly. Stamp out sixteen 4-inch circles, using a biscuit cutter or small saucer, re-rolling the dough as necessary. Spoon 2 teaspoons of the lamb filling into the center of each dough circle. Brush the edges of the dough with some of the remaining egg and fold the dough over to form semicircles. Press to seal.

Transfer the pastries to a lightly greased baking tray, brush with more egg, and bake for 20 to 25 minutes, until golden. Serve warm with wedges of lemon and a crisp salad.

CHAPTER TWO

MEAT AND POULTRY

Blends of spices lend magically
different flavors to cooked
meat and poultry, so the same basic
ingredients can take on a completely
new character. With a
well-stocked spice cupboard, you
can produce meat and poultry dishes
reflecting the diversity of the
world's cuisines.

MEAT AND POULTRY

Whether you roast or broil meat, or slow-cook a warming casserole or stew, the addition of spices will make your meal more interesting and pleasurable. Traditional Spiced Beef, *marinated overnight in Port wine and allspice, and* Mustard-Glazed Ham, *stuck with cloves, bring to mind a Victorian Christmas feast.* In contrast, Chinese Red-Cooked Pork *with star anise, and* Fragrant Szechuan Crisp Roast Duck *with five-spice powder bring an oriental touch to your table. Almost every country possesses its own spicy stew or casserole dish: India has curries; Africa offers rich stews seasoned with fiery berbere, and tagines subtly flavored with cinnamon, coriander, and cumin. The Americas have given us chilies, and dishes such as gumbo, chili con carne, and* Chili-Beef Casserole.

Grace before meal, *Jan Steen, 17th century.*

TRADITIONAL SPICED BEEF

Spiced beef is a traditional British Christmas dish. It is enhanced with the mellow flavor of nutmeg and the pungency of allspice berries. Serve it hot with this rich port-wine gravy and red-currant jelly, accompanied by freshly cooked vegetables; it is equally delicious served cold, as part of a buffet, with a pot of horseradish sauce.

SERVES 8

3-pound piece beef tenderloin, trimmed
²/₃ cup port wine
4 tbsp red-wine vinegar
2 tbsp dark brown sugar
1 tbsp allspice berries, crushed
2 tbsp butter
1 tbsp vegetable oil

STUFFING
8 slices lean Canadian bacon, trimmed
2 tbsp grated beef suet
½ tsp grated nutmeg

2 tbsp chopped fresh parsley
½ tsp salt
2 cups fresh white bread crumbs
1 small egg, beaten

GRAVY
2 tbsp all-purpose flour
1¼ cups beef stock
²/₃ cup port wine
2 tbsp mushroom ketchup
Salt and freshly ground black pepper

First prepare the beef. Using a sharp knife, slice down the center of the beef lengthwise, to within 1 inch of the other side. Open the beef out and pound it with a meat mallet to tenderize. Put the beef in a large, shallow dish and pour the port wine, vinegar, sugar, and allspice over. Cover and chill overnight, turning occasionally.

The next day, heat the oven to 350°F. Make the stuffing. Chop 2 slices of the bacon and mix with the other stuffing ingredients to form a firm mixture. Remove the beef from the marinade and put the stuffing down the center of the beef. Roll up the beef and secure with skewers.

Melt the butter and oil in a large skillet and fry the beef joint for 4 to 5 minutes, until browned on all sides. Drain on paper towels, reserving the pan juices; set aside to cool. Wrap the remaining bacon over the length of the beef and secure with string. Place the beef on a roasting rack over a pan and pour the reserved pan juices over. Roast for 2 to 2½ hours, basting occasionally, until the beef is cooked to your liking. Let the beef stand, covered, while preparing the gravy.

Strain the cooking juices from the beef into a saucepan and blend with the flour to form a paste. Gradually stir in the stock, port wine, and mushroom ketchup. Heat, stirring, until thickened. Season to taste with salt and pepper.

To serve, discard the string from the beef and slice the meat. Serve with the gravy as an accompaniment.

CHILI-BEEF CASSEROLE

Chili meat dishes have their origins in Mexico, although the versions we are familiar with were probably created in the southwest. This hearty casserole combines the ingredients commonly used in many Mexican dishes and is flavored with hot spices, such as cayenne pepper and chilies, and earthy, woody spices, such as cinnamon and cloves. The amount of chili powder you add is up to you. Serve simply with boiled rice, a salad, and iced water or beer to put out the fire!

SERVES 4

1½ pounds lean braising steak, cut into 1-inch cubes
1 tbsp red-wine vinegar
1 tsp sugar
Salt and freshly ground black pepper
3 tbsp vegetable oil
1 large onion, chopped
2 garlic cloves, finely chopped
2 green chilies, seeded and finely chopped

1 cinnamon stick, broken
5 cloves
1 to 3 tsp chili powder
1 tsp cayenne pepper
1 tsp dried oregano
2 cups water
1 (14-oz.) can crushed tomatoes
2 tbsp tomato paste
1 can (14-oz.) red kidney beans, rinsed and drained

Mix the beef, vinegar, and sugar together. Season with salt and pepper; set aside to tenderize for 20 minutes.

Heat the oil in a large saucepan and gently fry the onion, garlic, chilies, spices, and oregano for 2 to 3 minutes, until the onion is just beginning to soften. Add the beef and cook, stirring, for 4 to 5 minutes, until the beef is browned all over. Pour in the water and bring to a boil. Cover and leave to simmer for an hour.

Mix in the crushed tomatoes, tomato paste, and kidney beans. Bring back to a boil and simmer, uncovered, for 30 minutes longer, until the beef is tender. Discard the cinnamon and cloves before serving.

JAMAICAN JERK PORK

There is no specific English meaning for the word "jerk," but it is believed to describe an ancient Arawak Indian method of cooking pork, which gives a kick to pork through the fiery seasoning, derived from chilies. The recipe has evolved over the years and still remains very popular throughout Jamaica. The pork is barbecued or broiled in the spicy sauce and is best served with boiled sweet potatoes or rice and a salad. Add the chili sauce to your liking!

SERVES 4

1½ pounds lean pork tenderloin, trimmed and cut into ½-inch thick slices
2 red chilies, seeded and finely chopped
1 onion, finely chopped
2 garlic cloves, finely chopped
1-inch piece of fresh gingerroot, peeled and finely chopped

1 to 2 tbsp bottled hot chili sauce
6 tbsp vegetable stock
1 tsp ground allspice
2 tbsp dark soy sauce
2 bay leaves
6 tbsp water

Put the pork slices in a shallow dish. Blend the chilies, onion, garlic, and ginger in a small blender to form a paste. Mix in the chili sauce, stock, allspice, and soy sauce. Pour over the pork and add the bay leaves. Cover and chill overnight, turning occasionally.

The next day, remove the pork from the marinade and barbecue over hot coals or put under a preheated medium broiler for 5 to 6 minutes on each side, until well cooked.

Pour the marinade into a small saucepan and add the water. Bring to a boil and simmer for 10 minutes, until reduced. Serve as a sauce to accompany the pork.

58

Marco Polo, 1254–1324

Marco Polo was the son of Nicolo Polo, a Venetian merchant and adventurer. In about 1260, Nicolo and his brother Maffeo went on an expedition to the court of Kublai Khan, leader of the Mongols and ruler of China. When they made a second journey to China some years later, they took the 15-year-old Marco with them. This time they were away for 26 years, but they returned home with untold wealth in jewels and fabrics, and many tales of the fabulous riches of China.

They also brought back spices and tales of spices. When dictating his memoirs, Marco Polo told of the 10,000 pounds of pepper eaten every day in the Chinese city of Hangchow, and of the vast plantations of nutmegs and cloves that he had seen in Java and in the islands in the China Sea. The more they listened to the tales of Marco Polo, the more the European merchants realized these places could be reached by sea–a fact that would help to end the Arab dominance of the spice trade.

CHINESE RED-COOKED PORK

Marinating tender, lean pork in a blend of soy sauce and five-spice powder gives this dish its rich color.

SERVES 4

1½ -pound piece of pork tenderloin
Scallion tassels and sliced carrot and pepper, to garnish
Soy sauce, to serve

MARINADE
6 tbsp light soy sauce
2 tbsp dry sherry

1 tbsp sugar
1 tsp five-spice powder
2 garlic cloves, crushed
1-inch piece of fresh gingerroot, peeled and finely chopped

GLAZE
⅓ cup sugar
6 tbsp red-wine vinegar

First prepare the pork and marinade. Put the pork tenderloin in a shallow dish. Mix the marinade ingredients together and pour over the pork. Cover and chill overnight, turning occasionally.

The next day, heat the oven to 350°F. Remove the pork from the marinade and put it on a rack over a roasting pan. Roast for an hour, basting with the marinade from time to time, until it is richly brown and cooked through.

Meanwhile, make the scallion tassels and the glaze. For the scallion tassels, trim the scallions into 3-inch lengths. Using a pair of small kitchen scissors, cut down the greenest part of the onion, stopping half-way down. Continue to snip the onion into strips. Place in a bowl of cold water in the refrigerater for about 30 minutes until curled. Drain and shake well to remove the excess water. For the glaze, put the sugar and vinegar in a small saucepan and heat gently to dissolve the sugar. Bring to a boil and simmer for 3 to 4 minutes, until syrupy.

As soon as the pork is cooked, brush it with the glaze and leave to stand, uncovered, for 5 minutes. Slice the pork thinly and arrange the slices on a warmed serving platter. Garnish with scallion tassels and sliced carrot and pepper. Serve with a bowl of soy sauce for dipping.

CHUTNEYS, PICKLES, AND SAUCES

DILL PICKLES

Dill pickles are a main ingredient of the perfect hot dog or burger. The sweet-sour combination, flavored with tangy spices, makes a delicious accompaniment to cold meats and salads.

MAKES ABOUT 4 POUNDS

2 large cucumbers, preferably ridge variety, thickly sliced
2 large onions, thickly sliced
4 tbsp coarse sea salt
Crushed ice
2½ cups cider vinegar
1 tsp ground turmeric
1 tbsp mustard seeds
6 cloves
½ tsp black peppercorns
2 bay leaves
Fresh dill sprigs
1¼ cups sugar

Place the cucumbers and onions in a large bowl and sprinkle with salt and crushed ice. Lay a plate on top of them and press down with a weight; set aside for 4 hours.

Meanwhile, pour the vinegar into a saucepan and add the turmeric, mustard seeds, cloves, and peppercorns. Tie the bay leaves and dill together with a clean piece of string and add to the pan with the sugar. Heat gently, stirring until the sugar dissolves. Remove from the heat and set aside to infuse for at least an hour.

Rinse and drain the cucumber and onion. Bring the vinegar to a boil and add the vegetables. Bring back to a boil and then remove from the heat. Discard the herbs. Ladle into warmed, sterilized (see below) preserving jars and seal. Label and store in a cool dark place for 2 weeks before using. Store in the refrigerator after opening.

TO STERILIZE JARS FOR PRESERVING

Stand the jars on a wire rack in a saucepan and pour over sufficient water to cover. Bring to a boil, cover, and boil for 15 minutes. Dip any lids in boiling water, to sterilize them before using, as well.

LEMON PICKLE

Serve this with fried vegetables and snacks. The recipe originates from Kenya, where pickle is called *achar*. It is fragrant from saffron and hot from red chilies. Let the pickle stand for a week before using it and serving it with firm white barbecued fish.

MAKES ABOUT 1½ POUNDS

8 lemons, scrubbed
4 tbsp coarse salt
2 tsp mustard seeds
Saffron strands
3 fresh red chilies, seeded and finely chopped
⅔ cup sunflower oil

Thinly slice 4 lemons. Put them in a bowl and sprinkle with the salt; set aside.

Pare the peel from the remaining lemons, using a vegetable peeler, and slice into thin strips. Put the lemon peel in a small heatproof bowl and pour over sufficient boiling water just to cover; set aside for 5 minutes.

Meanwhile, grind the mustard seeds, chilies, and a large pinch of saffron strands in a mortar with pestle. Transfer to a large bowl and stir in the oil.

Drain the lemon slices and the peel and add to the spice oil. Mix together until well coated. Transfer to a sterilized preserving jar and seal. Label and store in the refrigerator for a week before using. Once open, keep refrigerated.

60

MANGO CHUTNEY

Chutneys are ideal for serving with curries, cold meats, and cheeses. The recipe uses the classic pickling spice mix on page 81, which contains pungent aromatic spices, such as mustard, chili, black pepper, cloves, and allspice. It is best to use slightly underripe mangoes for a firmer result.

MAKES ABOUT 5 POUNDS

1½ cups finely chopped onions
2 garlic cloves, finely chopped
1 fresh red chili, seeded and finely chopped
6 large, underripe mangoes, peeled, seeded, and chopped
2 tsp pickling spice (see page 81)
1¼ cups white-wine vinegar
Finely grated peel and juice of 1 small orange
1¾ cups plus 2 tbsp sugar
Salt and freshly ground black pepper (optional)

Put the onions, garlic, and chili into a preserving pan or very large saucepan. Add half the mango and stir. Tie the pickling spice in a small cheesecloth bag and add to the saucepan, with the vinegar. Bring to a boil and leave to simmer gently for 20 minutes. Stir in the orange peel and juice and remaining mango. Cook for 5 minutes longer. Stir in the sugar and continue stirring over low heat, until dissolved. Bring to a boil and boil steadily for 15 minutes, until the consistency is like a soft jam; the last addition of mango should hold its shape. Season to taste. Remove from the heat and set aside for 10 minutes. Discard the shice bag. Transfer to sterilized jars (see page 60) and then seal label and use within 6 months.

CRANBERRY CHUTNEY

This is a delicious sweet chutney and makes an excellent alternative to cranberry sauce with turkey. The recipe uses a lot of pickling spice with pungent flavors from mustard, chili, black pepper, cloves, and allspice. If you prefer a milder flavor, reduce the quantity of spice added.

MAKES ABOUT 3 POUNDS

5 cups peeled, cored, and chopped cooking apples
2½ cups cranberries
1 tbsp pickling spice (see page 81)
2 cinnamon sticks
1¼ cups cider vinegar
1¾ cups plus 2 tbsp light brown sugar
1 cup seedless raisins
Salt and freshly ground black pepper

Put the apples and cranberries in a large saucepan. Tie the pickling spices in a small cheesecloth bag and add to the fruit, with the cinnamon and vinegar. Cover the pan—cranberries have a tendency to "pop" during cooking—bring to a boil and cook gently for 15 minutes, until softened.

Remove the lid and stir in the sugar over low heat, until dissolved. Add the raisins and bring to a boil. Boil steadily for 15 minutes, until thick and jamlike in consistency. Season lightly. Discard the pickling spices and cinnamon sticks. Spoon into hot, sterilized jars (see page 60) and seal. Label and store until required.

CHICKEN KORMA

This Indian dish is a mild, creamy curry, flavored with a blend of subtle, fragrant spices, including cinnamon, coriander, and cardamom. The yogurt and coconut tenderizes the chicken, as well as adding creaminess to the sauce. Look for bars of creamed coconut in oriental grocery stores.

SERVES 4

1½ cups chopped onions
1-inch piece of fresh ginger, peeled and chopped
3 garlic cloves, peeled and chopped
3 tbsp vegetable ghee or 3 tbsp butter, melted
1½ pounds boneless, skinless chicken breasts, cut into 1½-inch cubes
1 tbsp ground coriander
1 cinnamon stick, broken
5 cardamom pods
Juice of 1 small lemon
1 tsp salt
Freshly ground black pepper
⅓ cup blanched almonds, very finely ground

2 ounces creamed coconut, grated
⅔ cup plain yogurt
⅔ cup water

SALAD
4-inch piece of cucumber, rinsed and finely diced
4 tomatoes, chopped
1 onion, peeled and finely chopped
2 tbsp freshly chopped mint

TO SERVE
4 cups hot cooked turmeric rice
¼ cup slivered almonds, toasted
2 tbsp chopped fresh cilantro

Put the onions, ginger, and garlic in a small blender or food processor and blend for a few seconds to form a smooth paste. Heat the ghee or melted butter in a large skillet. Add the onion paste and fry, stirring, for 2 to 3 minutes, until softened but not golden.

Add the chicken and cook, stirring, for 5 to 6 minutes longer, until lightly browned all over. Stir in all the spices, lemon juice, salt, and season with pepper. Continue to cook, stirring occasionally, for 10 minutes. Stir in the ground almonds and coconut.

Gradually add the yogurt, a spoonful at a time, stirring continuously to blend into the mixture. Cook for a minute longer, until thick. Pour in the water, just to cover the chicken. Simmer gently for 15 to 20 minutes, until cooked through. Discard the cinnamon stick and cardamom pods.

This dish is ideal served with turmeric yellow rice and a salad of chopped cucumber, tomato, onion, and mint. Chop the salad ingredients. Mix them together, cover, and chill until required.

For a special presentation, transfer the curry to a warmed serving platter lined with cooked rice. Sprinkle with slivered almonds and chopped cilantro and serve with the chilled salad.

Hippocras

During medieval times, spices were often added to wines to improve the flavor of what were perhaps poor vintages. People developed a taste for these spiced wines and they became a specialty. During the 14th and 15th centuries, a spiced wine called Hippocras was popular. It acquired its name from the practice of filtering the spice-infused wine through a conical bag, which resembled the sleeve of the gown worn by physicians of the time. The bag was known as "Hippocrates' sleeve," named after the ancient Greek father of medicine, whose Hippocratic oath newly qualified doctors took then, as they still do today. Hippocras usually had a red-wine base, and was flavored with a variety of spices. Ginger, cinnamon, and grains-of-paradise were the most popular, and, in wealthy houses, the wine was sweetened with sugar. The poor, if they could get wine at all, substituted pepper for grains-of-paradise and used home-produced honey as a sweetener. Both red and white hippocras were still drunk in the 18th century. To make the white version, milk or cream was added to white wine, along with the spices and sugar.

CHICKEN GUMBO

Everyone in the state of Louisiana has their own version of a gumbo. It is a classic Creole dish, with its hint of Spanish, African, and native-American flavors. Its name derives from the Bantu word for okra, an essential ingredient. This chicken gumbo is flavored with a traditional Cajun spice mixture of paprika, cumin, cayenne, black pepper, and thyme.

SERVES 4

1 tbsp corn oil
4 ounces chorizo sausage, chopped
1 large onion, sliced
2 celery sticks, chopped
3 cups trimmed and sliced okra
1 can (14-oz.) crushed tomatoes
2 garlic cloves, finely chopped
1 tbsp Cajun seasoning (see page 81), or 1 tbsp commercial Cajun seasoning
2 tbsp butter

2 tbsp all-purpose flour
2½ cups chicken stock
6 ounces shelled uncooked shrimp, thawed if frozen
3 cups cooked and skinned chicken, cut into 1-inch pieces
Hot-pepper sauce

To Serve
1 cup long-grain rice
2 tbsp chopped fresh celery leaves

Heat the oil in a skillet and gently fry the sausage for 2 to 3 minutes, until light golden. Add the onion and celery and cook for 3 to 4 minutes longer, until softened. Stir in the okra and gently fry for 3 minutes. Stir in the tomatoes, garlic, and seasoning and simmer for 15 minutes.

Meanwhile, melt the butter and mix in the flour. Cook, stirring, until the mixture turns golden brown. Gradually stir in the stock. Pour over the okra mixture and bring to a boil. Cover and leave to simmer for an hour.

Cook the rice in boiling, salted water according to the package directions. Drain and keep hot.

Stir in the shrimp and chicken and cook 5 minutes longer. Stir in a few drops of hot-pepper sauce. Spoon the gumbo into serving bowls lined with hot cooked rice and some chopped fresh celery leaves.

DORO WOT

This is a thick, traditional Ethiopian chicken stew, flavored with chilies and an African spice mix called *berbere*. *Berbere* spice mix is strong in flavor and reminiscent of Madras curry powder. The spices included in the blend are dried chilies, coriander, cloves, cardamom, black pepper, ajowan (or substitute dried thyme), and fenugreek. The latter two, less familiar, spices are widely used in Indian cookery: ajowan tastes similar to thyme and fenugreek has a strong aroma of celery and a bitter taste. Serve this stew with warmed African or pita bread to mop up the juices.

SERVES 4

½ cup butter	*2 cups chicken stock*
4 large onions, chopped	*2 pounds chicken pieces*
2 garlic cloves, finely chopped	*4 medium eggs, hard-boiled*
1 cup tomato paste	*and shelled*
½ cup water	
2 tsp berbere *spice mix*	TO SERVE
(see page 81)	*African or pita bread, warmed*
Salt and freshly ground black	*Chopped fresh cilantro*
pepper	

Melt the butter in a heavy-bottomed skillet or saucepan and gently fry the onions and garlic for 10 minutes, until soft and golden. Stir the tomato paste with the water and pour this into the onions with the *berbere* spices. Season with salt and pepper. Pour in the stock and bring to a boil. Leave to simmer for 10 minutes.

Prick the chicken pieces all over, using a fork, and put them in the simmering sauce, making sure they are well covered. Continue to simmer for 30 minutes.

Prick the eggs all over and add to the chicken. Continue to cook for 15 minutes longer, until the chicken is tender and the sauce is thick. Serve sprinkled with cilantro and accompanied by warmed African or pita bread.

Mustard-Glazed Ham

This is equally delicious served hot as a roast, with roasted vegetables and apple sauce, or cold as part of a buffet table. The meat is penetrated by the earthy, warm aromatic flavor of cloves, the unopened buds of a small evergreen tree native to Indonesia. Allow plenty of time to prepare this recipe—the ham needs soaking overnight to help extract the saltiness.

SERVES 8

3½-pound boneless ham joint, tied with string and soaked overnight in cold water
2 bay leaves
1 onion, quartered
½ cup brown sugar
About 60 cloves

8 juniper berries
8 black peppercorns
1 cinnamon stick, broken
2 tbsp red-wine vinegar
1 tbsp honey
2 tbsp wholegrain mustard

Drain the ham and put it in a large saucepan with the bay leaves, onion, and 2 tbsp sugar. Place 8 cloves, the juniper berries, peppercorns, and cinnamon in a clean piece of cheesecloth and tie with string. Add to the saucepan. Pour in sufficient cold water to cover the ham. Bring to a boil, remove the scum from the surface with a flat ladle. Cover, reduce the heat, and simmer gently for 1 hour.

Heat the oven to 350°F. Place a large sheet of foil in a roasting pan. Drain the ham and stand it on the foil. Fold over the ends of the foil to cover the ham. Bake for 25 minutes.

Discard the foil and string. Strip away the brown skin, exposing the white fat. Using a sharp knife, score the fat in a crisscross pattern and press a clove into each diamond.

Heat the vinegar, honey, and mustard until melted. Brush generously over the fat. Sprinkle with the remaining sugar. Return the ham to the oven and bake for 40 minutes longer, until golden. If serving hot, leave to rest for at least 10 minutes before you carve.

Chilies

USED IN THE AMERICAS FOR MANY CENTURIES BEFORE COLUMBUS, CHILIES—THE FRUITS OF VARIETIES OF CAPSICUM FRUTESCENS—HAVE BECOME THE MOST COMMON SPICE IN MANY COUNTRIES.

Chili paste was a popular ingredient of gravies and sauces in Victorian England.

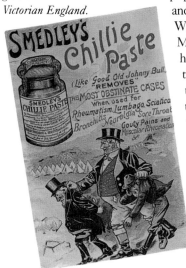

The word chili comes from the language of the early inhabitants of Mexico and Central America. These hot, spicy peppers have been eaten in both countries and in South America for at least 9,000 years. When Christopher Columbus reached Mexico he found what the Italian historian Peter Martyr described at the time as, "peppers more pungent than that from Caucasus." Many years prior to then, the Arawaks and Caribs had taken chilies with them when they migrated from what is now Venezuela to the West Indies. Columbus had encountered the peppers in Hispaniola (Haiti) and in Cuba in 1492.

In the 16th century, Spanish and Portuguese conquerors carried *Capsicum frutescens* plants back to Europe. Chilies became established in Spain and Portugal and then traveled to India via the Arab spice routes, being adapted into many local cuisines alone the way. Varieties were developed to produce the large sweet peppers that we use as vegetables and also the smaller, dark red *Capsicum annuum*, which is ground to make

At this Indian pepper market, the traders sit among the piles of brightly-colored spices.

paprika. Chilies are now cultivated by the majority of spice-producing countries. They flourish in warm, humid climates, where they are grown mostly as annuals, picked when ripe and sold either fresh or dried. Some varieties are ground into chili powder or dried cayenne pepper. Across the world there is a huge choice of chilies of different colors, sizes and strengths of flavor.

The hotness of chilies is due to a substance called capsaicin and the hotter varieties may contain from 0.2 to 1 percent, which is mainly concentrated in the area where the seeds are attached to the central portion. The small, thin-skinned chilies, such as those known as "devil peppers" and "bird's-eye peppers" generally have the highest capsaicin content. Other hot varieties include jalapeno, tabasco, cayenne, ancho, Japanese Santaka, and Hontaka, and Bombay cherries.

CHILI PRODUCTS

Cayenne pepper is the ground, dried powder from the smaller, hotter chilies that are grown in Mexico, Louisiana, India, Africa, China and Japan. These vary in color from orange-red to brown and are usually very hot.

Red pepper is a name sometimes applied to cayenne pepper, but it also refers to a slightly milder form of ground chili that is produced in the United States and Turkey.

Crushed red pepper, also known as *peperone rosso* or "pizza pepper," is a pungent seasoning made from a mixture of different varieties of *Capsicum frutescens*. It is mainly used in sausages and manufactured products.

Chili powder is said to have been invented in the 1860s by an English immigrant to the United States who wanted a substitute for curry powder. However, the Aztecs were using a similar blend at the time of the Spanish conquest. Wherever it came from, chili powder was frequently used in pioneering days by chuck wagon cooks on cattle drives, who found it useful in preserving their meat, and who are said to have invented chili con carne, partly

Cayenne

This is the most acrid and stimulating spice with which we are aquainted [sic]... All the pods are extremely pungent to the taste and in the green state are used by us as a pickle. When ripe, they are ground into cayenne pepper, and sold as a condiment. The best of this, however, is made in the West Indies, from what is called the Bird pepper, on account of hens and turkeys being extremely partial to it.

ISABELLA BEETON, *BEETON'S BOOK OF HOUSEHOLD MANAGEMENT, 1859*

as a result. Commercial chili powder contains ground chilies, plus oregano cumin, garlic powder, and other spices.

Tabasco sauce is a red-hot and red-colored liquid, made from tabasco peppers, which can give a dash of piquancy to soups, sauces, and casseroles, and to the tomato juice drink called Bloody Mary. The latter was invented in 1920 by Ferdinand Petoit, the bartender at Harry's New York Bar in Paris.

PREPARING FRESH CHILIES
Remove the cores with a small, pointed knife. Slice the chilies in half lengthwise and scrape out and discard the seeds. Do not let the juice squirt in your eyes and do not lick your fingers or rub your eyes after handling chilies. Wash your hands, the knife and the chopping board after preparation.

MEDICINAL USES
Chilies stimulate the flow of saliva and digestive juices, so they have been used as a remedy for loss of appetite and other digestive troubles. An infusion of dried or ground chilies, or a pinch of cayenne pepper in hot water, is a good remedy for chills and fever. Chili oil is an ingredient of ointments and rubs for rheumatism.

Strings of chilies hanging up to dry outside a house in Santa Fe, New Mexico (above left).

There are many different colors, sizes, and shapes of chili. These thin red ones are ready for picking.

STUFFED TURKEY *and* SPICY RED CABBAGE

Red cabbage steeped in vinegar, sugar, and such pungent spices as cloves and juniper makes a wonderful complement to rich meats like venison or goose. It is a very festive dish and is ideal served as part of an alternative Thanksgiving meal. Here, a turkey breast joint is stuffed with a tasty mixture seasoned with nutmeg and orange, accompanied by the cabbage.

SERVES 4

3-pound turkey breast joint
2 tbsp butter, softened
6 slices bacon

STUFFING
10 ounces sausagemeat
1 tsp grated orange peel
½ tsp grated nutmeg
1 small onion, minced
1 tsp Italian seasoning
Salt and freshly ground black
    pepper

CABBAGE
4 tbsp butter
1 large onion, finely shredded
3 cups peeled, cored, and thinly
    sliced cooking apples
1 red cabbage, finely shredded
1 tbsp juniper berries, crushed
½ tsp ground cloves
4 tbsp dark brown sugar
3 tbsp red-wine vinegar
6 tbsp water
Salt and freshly ground black
    pepper

Heat the oven to 375°F. First prepare the turkey. Mix the sausagemeat, orange peel, nutmeg, onion, and herbs together and season with salt and pepper. Fill the neck end of the turkey joint and truss with string. Weigh the turkey and calculate the cooking time at 25 minutes per pound plus 25 minutes. (For example, a 3-pound bird, including stuffing, will take 1 hour 40 minutes.) Put the turkey in a roasting pan.

Spread the skin with the softened butter and arrange bacon slices over the turkey in a crisscross pattern. Bake, basting occasionally and covering with foil once the turkey is well browned, until the juices run clear. Stand, covered, for 15 minutes before carving.

Meanwhile, cook the cabbage. Melt the butter in a large saucepan and gently fry the onion and apples, stirring, for 3 to 4 minutes, until well coated in butter and just softening. Add the cabbage, spices, sugar, vinegar, and water, then season with salt and pepper and stir. Bring to a boil. Cover and leave to simmer for 15 minutes, until tender. Drain.

Transfer the turkey to a warmed platter, and serve with the cabbage, roast potatoes, and Brussels sprouts.

MOUSSAKA

This delicately flavoured lamb and eggplant bake from Greece is seasoned with cinnamon. It is a very rich dish and is best served with a salad and some fresh, crusty bread. It is important to prepare the eggplant carefully, making sure you wash as much salt from them as possible, otherwise the saltiness will dominate the dish and the other flavors will not come through.

SERVES 4

*2 pounds eggplants, thinly
  sliced*
4 tbsp salt
7 tbsp olive oil
2 garlic cloves, crushed
2 red onions, finely chopped
1 pound ground lamb
1 cinnamon stick, broken
1 tsp dried oregano
*1 can (14-oz.) crushed
  tomatoes*

2 tbsp tomato paste
Freshly ground black pepper

SAUCE
4 tbsp butter or margarine
Scant ½ cup all-purpose flour
2½ cups milk
1 medium egg yolk, beaten
*4 tbsp freshly grated Parmesan
  cheese*
4 tbsp fresh white bread crumbs

Layer the eggplants in a large bowl, sprinkling with salt as you go; set aside for 30 minutes to draw out the bitter juices from the eggplant. Then rinse the eggplants well in cold, running water to remove the salt and juices, and pat dry with paper towels.

Heat the oven to 350°F. Heat 6 tablespoons of oil in a large skillet and gently fry the garlic and eggplant slices for 5 to 6 minutes, until softened and lightly browned; drain and set aside. Heat the remaining oil and gently fry the onions and lamb for 3 to 4 minutes, until the lamb is browned all over. Add the cinnamon stick, oregano, tomatoes, and tomato paste. Season with pepper. Bring to a boil. Simmer gently for 40 minutes until thick and tender.

Meanwhile, to make the sauce, melt the butter or margarine in a saucepan. Stir in the flour and cook for a minute. Remove from the heat and gradually blend in the milk. Return to the heat, stir until the sauce thickens to a pouring consistency. Remove from the heat and stir in the egg yolk; set aside.

Layer the eggplants in the bottom of a baking dish. Season with black pepper. Discard the cinnamon stick from the lamb mixture and spoon it over the eggplants. Top with the sauce. Sprinkle with cheese and bread crumbs and stand the dish on a baking tray. Bake for 50 minutes. Let the moussaka stand for 10 minutes before serving.

FRAGRANT SZECHWAN CRISP ROAST DUCK

Szechwan peppercorns, or *fagara,* are reddish in color, with a mildly hot flavor and a spicy fragrance similar to coriander seeds. It is one of the oldest-established spices in China and is an excellent seasoning for poultry and meat. Here, the peppercorns are crushed with the mildly aniseed flavor of star anise and brushed over the duck.

SERVES 4

5-pound oven-ready duck	⅔ cup water
1 tbsp Szechwan peppercorns (fagara)	Sliced fresh chilies, to garnish
2 star anise	To Serve
1 tsp ground ginger	Chinese pancakes
1 tbsp dark soy sauce	Bottled hoisin sauce
1 tbsp honey	Shredded scallions and
1 tbsp rice wine	cucumber strips

Bring a large saucepan of water to a boil. Add the duck, breast-side down, and hold under water using a spoon for 30 seconds. Remove the duck and dry immediately with paper towels. Put it on a tray and chill overnight in the bottom of the refrigerator, uncovered, so the skin dries out.

The next day, heat the oven to 375°F. Prick the duck all over with a fork. Pound the Szechwan peppercorns and star anise to a powder in a mortar and pestle (or grind them in an electric grinder). Mix with the ginger. Mix together the soy sauce, honey, and rice wine and brush some over the duck. Sprinkle with half the spices and chill for 1 hour longer, for the flavors to develop.

Put the duck on a roasting rack, breast-side up, over a large pan. Pour the water into the pan and bake for 1½ hours.

Turn the duck over, brush it again with the soy sauce mixture, and sprinkle with the remaining spices. Bake for 1 hour longer.

Raise the oven temperature to 425°F. Turn the duck over again and bake for 20 to 25 minutes, until the skin is dark and crisp and the juices run clear.

Put the duck on a warmed serving platter and garnish with fresh chilies. Shred the duck and place a little on each pancake, with hoisin sauce, shredded scallions, and strips of cucumber. Roll up the pancakes to serve.

LAMB TAGINE

Tagines originate in Morocco and take their name from the wide dishes with conical lids they are cooked in. They are very aromatic and often contain sweetmeats, such as dried fruit, seeds, nuts, and honey. The spices used—cinnamon, coriander, and cumin—enhance the sweetness of the dish and complement the richness of the lamb. Traditionally, tagines are served on a bed of freshly steamed and buttered couscous.

SERVES 4

1½ pounds lean, boneless lamb, cut into 1-inch cubes	4 ounces dried prunes
4 tbsp butter, melted	4 ounces no-need-to-soak dried apricots
2 tbsp olive oil	1 small lemon, scrubbed
2 tsp ground cumin	2 tbsp honey
2 tsp ground coriander	
1 tbsp ground cinnamon	
2 red onions, finely chopped	To Garnish
1 tbsp lemon juice	2 tbsp sesame seeds, toasted
2 garlic cloves, finely chopped	2 tbsp chopped fresh cilantro
Salt and freshly ground black pepper	

Put the lamb in a bowl and stir in the melted butter, oil, spices, onions, lemon juice, and garlic. Season with salt and pepper. Transfer to a large saucepan and cook, stirring, for 4 to 5 minutes, to brown the meat. Pour in enough water to cover the meat, bring to a boil, and simmer gently, partially covered, for 1½ hours until the meat is tender.

Stir in the prunes and apricots. Using a vegetable peeler, pare the peel from the lemon and stir it into the meat with the honey. Bring back to a boil and simmer, uncovered, for 30 minutes longer, until the sauce has reduced.

Pile onto a serving dish, which you can line with freshly steamed couscous, and sprinkle with the sesame seeds and chopped cilantro.

CHAPTER THREE

FISH AND SHELLFISH

*T*he delicate qualities of
fish and shellfish are
wonderfully enhanced by subtle
combinations of spices that
complement and do not mask flavors.
Using different blends, you can
produce authentic fish dishes
from around the world.

FISH AND SHELLFISH

Fish and shellfish can be sautéed in butter or oil, broiled, added to rice or pasta for a complete main dish, or ground and formed into small cakes. Cod Steaks with a Peppercorn Crust *and* Cajun Blackened Fish *are made by coating fish in spices before gently frying it, but the flavors are totally dissimilar. The former combines different colored peppercorns with a cream sauce, and the latter uses a fiery mixture of Cajun spices. Tuna steaks are marinated with wine, mustard seeds, pepper and cayenne pepper before being broiled and served with harissa, a sauce made from hot red chilies, to make* Tuna Steaks with Pepper Sauce. Cuban Fish and Rice with Rum *is an unusual rice dish, flavored with saffron.* White fish cakes *are given a Thai twist with lime, red chilies, and fresh ginger. Succulent shrimp are wonderful served in a coconut curry or broiled with* piri-piri, *a hot chili sauce from Portugal.*

Fish and fishing from Graphic Illustrations of Animals,
Thomas Varty, London, c. 1850.

CAJUN BLACKENED FISH

Down in the southern states, there is a real melting-pot of influences, from Spanish-, French-, and African-Americans, which gives us the unique flavors of Cajun and Creole cooking. The idea of "blackening" food was invented in New Orleans; it involves sealing the food in a spice crust. Here, lightly flavored white fish is cooked in a blend of Cajun spices and herbs, such as paprika, cumin, cayenne, black pepper, and dried thyme. Blackened fish is perfect served with a squeeze of lemon juice, some boiled rice, and a crisp salad.

SERVES 4

4 white fish fillets, such as flounder, cod or bass, each weighing 6 ounces and about ½ inch thick
4 tbsp butter, melted

1 quantity Cajun seasoning (see page 81), or 3 tbsp commercial Cajun seasoning
Lemon wedges, to serve

Wash and pat dry the fish fillets. Dip them in the melted butter and sprinkle each side with the Cajun seasoning.

Put a heavy-based skillet (cast iron is ideal) on the range to heat slowly, until it is very hot. Hold the palm of your hand just above the surface to feel a strong, rising heat.

Press the fish fillets down firmly onto the skillet bottom, using a metal spatula: the fish will hiss and steam. Cook for 1 to 2 minutes, until blackened. Turn over and cook 1 to 2 minutes longer, until cooked through. Pour any remaining butter over to serve and accompany with a wedge of lemon to squeeze over the fish.

Punch

Punch has been a favorite drink in Britain and other Western countries since the 17th century. The term is usually applied to a mixture of wine and fruit juices heated with spices and chopped fruits. The idea came from India, where a similar drink had been prepared for about 2,000 years, via the merchants of the East India Company. The name that was exported with it derives from the Hindu word punch, *meaning "five," which referred to its five main ingredients: water, citron juice, sugar, spirits, and spice or other aromatic flavorings. The citron is similar to a lemon but less acid.*

At first, lime juice was a favorite Western replacement for the citron juice. Limes were grown in Jamaica and, from about 1680, the juice was extracted at source and exported in barrels to Europe. Many British country households developed their own punch recipes, and the juice was frequently omitted in favor of wine. A simple recipe of the time called for "one quart of claret wine, half a pint of brandy, and a little nutmeg grated, a little sugar, and the juice of a lemon." Many punch recipes have not changed since.

COD STEAKS *with a* PEPPERCORN CRUST

Peppercorns are the most widely used spice in the West, giving a warm, woody, aromatic flavor to food. Here, the spice enlivens a lightly flavored fish with a deliciously pungent crust and creamy sauce. Pink peppercorns have a more aromatic flavor than the others, and add a splash of color to the dish. This rich dish is best served simply with a salad or freshly cooked vegetables.

SERVES 4

4 cod fillet steaks, each weighing 6 ounces, skinned
4 tbsp butter, melted
2 tsp black peppercorns
2 tsp pink peppercorns
2 tsp white peppercorns
2 tbsp all-purpose flour
2 tbsp olive oil
²⁄₃ cup heavy cream
1 tbsp green peppercorns in brine, drained and rinsed
½ tsp salt
2 tbsp snipped fresh chives

Rinse the fish steaks and pat them dry with paper towels. Brush the fish on both sides with melted butter.

Finely crush the dry peppercorns in a mortar and pestle. Mix with the flour and put on a plate. Lightly coat the fish on both sides with the peppered flour.

Heat the remaining butter with the oil in a skillet. Fry the fish for 3 to 4 minutes on each side, until golden and just cooked through. Drain the fish steaks, reserving the pan juices, and keep them warm. Pour the cream into the juices and add the whole green peppercorns and salt. Bring to a boil and leave to simmer for 3 to 4 minutes, until thickened and reduced. Stir in the chives. Spoon over the cod to serve. Accompany with a salad or vegetables.

CUBAN FISH *and* RICE *with* RUM

There are obvious Spanish influences in Cuba and this is reflected in Cuban food. This recipe is similar to a paella but with the addition of dark rum and the warming spiciness of cumin, cinnamon, and saffron, which complement the seafood. This is a very hearty dish, a real meal-in-one, and needs only a crisp salad or crusty bread to accompany it.

SERVES 4

1 pound skinless, firm white fish fillets, such as cod, halibut, or monkfish, cut into chunks
1 tsp ground cumin
1 tsp dried oregano
4 tsp ground cinnamon
Juice of 1 large lemon
Salt and freshly ground black pepper
Generous 1¼ cups long-grain rice

5 cups fish or vegetable stock
2 tbsp vegetable oil
3 garlic cloves, finely chopped
1 large onion, chopped
1 red bell pepper, seeded and chopped
1 green bell pepper, seeded and chopped
1 yellow bell pepper, seeded and chopped
⅔ cup dark rum
Large pinch of saffron

Put the fish in a shallow dish and stir in the cumin, oregano, cinnamon, and lemon juice. Season with salt and pepper. Cover and chill for 2 hours. Meanwhile, put the rice in a bowl, pour half the stock over, cover, and chill.

Heat the oil in a large skillet. Add the garlic, onion, and peppers and fry for 3 to 4 minutes, until just softened. Add the fish and marinade and cook, stirring, for 2 minutes. Pour in the remaining stock, the soaked rice and its stock, the rum, and saffron, and season well. Bring to a boil, cover, and leave to simmer for 15 to 20 minutes, stirring occasionally and taking care not to break up the fish, until the fish is cooked through and the rice is tender.

Thai-Style Fish Cakes

These delicious little morsels are called *tod man pla* in Thailand. They are hot and fragrant, and typical of the cooking of that part of the world. Dried red chilies provide heat, and gingerroot and lime give fragrance. These deep-fried fish cakes are served with a slightly sour dipping sauce, flavored with the milder green chili.

MAKES 16 TO 20

1 pound firm white fish fillets, such as cod, haddock, or monkfish, skinned
4 dried red chilies, seeded and finely chopped
1 shallot, finely chopped
2 garlic cloves, finely chopped
1 tbsp chopped fresh cilantro
1-inch piece of fresh ginger, peeled and finely chopped
1 tsp grated lime peel
½ tsp salt
1 tbsp bottled fish sauce (nam pla)

Oil for deep-frying
Fresh red chili strips and kaffir lime leaves, to garnish

DIPPING SAUCE
6 tbsp lime juice
1 tbsp light brown sugar
1 tsp fish sauce (nam pla)
1 small shallot, finely chopped
1 fresh green chili, seeded and finely chopped

For the dipping sauce, mix all the ingredients together; set aside. Check the fish fillets for any remaining bones, then grind the fillets in a food processor or with a hand grinder. Put the ground fish in a bowl and combine it with the dried chilies, shallot, garlic, cilantro, ginger, lime peel, salt, and fish sauce, kneading to form a firm paste. Divide the mixture into 16 to 20 portions and form each into a small, flat cake, about 2½ inches in diameter and no more than ½ inch thick.

Heat the oil for deep-frying to 350°F, or until a cube of day-old bread browns in 30 seconds. Deep-fry the cakes 4 or 5 at a time for 2 to 3 minutes, until golden brown. Take care not to cook them too quickly, or they will become tough. Drain on paper towels. Garnish and serve warm, with the dipping sauce.

Christopher Columbus 1451–1506

Christopher Columbus was the son of a Genoese weaver, but it was to the Portuguese King John that he appealed for sponsorship of an expedition to reach the Spice Islands. When he was refused, he turned to King Ferdinand and Queen Isabella of Spain, who, only too pleased to outdo their competitor, appointed Columbus "Admiral of the Ocean Sea," and instructed him to bring back spices from the land of the "Great Khan."

On his first voyage, Columbus did not achieve his goal, but neither did he return empty-handed. Instead of finding the Spice Islands, with their plantations of pepper, cinnamon, and nutmeg, he came upon the island of Cuba, where there were chilies, yams, kidney beans, corn, cassava, and tobacco. On his second voyage, he came across allspice in the Caribbean, and on his third he found vanilla and cocoa beans in Mexico.

All these commodities eventually made their way back to Europe, where they influenced the cooking of many races, but Columbus never fulfilled his dream of finding a source of sweet spices and, hence, wealth for Spain. He died in 1506, on his fourth voyage, after finding his way westward blocked by the Isthmus of Panama.

79

SPICE BLENDS

FIVE-SPICE POWDER

This is one of the most delicious and fragrant blends, used throughout southern China and Vietnam. The basic five spices often have at least one other added to enhance the flavors. It is excellent with fish or poultry.

1 tbsp star anise
1 tbsp Szechwan peppercorns
  (fagara)
1 tbsp fennel seeds

1 small piece of cinnamon,
  flaked
½ tbsp cloves

Simply grind all the spices together to form a powder. Store in an air-tight jar for up to 3 months.

HARISSA

This hot chili sauce is used widely throughout Tunisia, Morocco, Libya, and Algeria in native recipes and as a relish served separately. It can be purchased from most Indian, African, and Middle Eastern food stores. Ask for "harissa sauce for couscous."

2 ounces dried red chilies
1 garlic clove
1 tbsp warm water
1 tsp coarse sea salt

1 tsp coriander seeds
1 tsp caraway seeds
½ tsp cumin seeds

Halve the chilies and remove the seeds and stems. Put in a large bowl and pour the warm water over; set aside to soak for 30 minutes. Drain them and put in a small blender or mortar and pestle, with the garlic, water, salt, and seeds. Bend or pound to form a paste. Transfer to a jar and refrigerate for up to 6 weeks.

PUDDING SPICE

A comforting, warming, sweet mixture from the British cooking tradition, used in cakes, puddings, and cookies. You can alter quantities to suit your taste.

1 tbsp each of the following:
  cloves, mace, grated nutmeg,
  allspice berries, and
  coriander seeds

1 small piece of cinnamon,
  flaked

Simply grind all the spices together to form a powder. Store in an air-tight jar for up to 3 months.

PICKLING SPICE

A traditional British blend used in the making of chutneys, pickled fruits and vegetables, and vinegars. The spices are either tied in a cheesecloth bag and discarded after use or added separately and left to steep in the liquid.

2 tbsp yellow mustard seeds
10 small dried red chilies
2 tbsp black peppercorns
2 tbsp allspice

1 tbsp cloves
1 small piece of dried
  gingerroot, coarsely grated

Tie the spices in a small, clean square of cheesecloth and add to the recipe as instructed—this will usually be the preferred method in chutney-making.

Alternatively, add the individual spices directly to the pickling liquid—this technique is more usual when making pickled fruit and vegetables or spiced vinegars.

BERBERE SPICE MIX

Traditional flavoring for Ethiopian _wots_, or stews. It is very similar to the strong flavors of an Indian Madras mix.

10 dried red chilies, chopped
½ tsp coriander seeds
5 cloves
seeds from 6 cardamom pods
¼ tsp ajowan seeds
8 allspice berries

½ tsp black peppercorns
½ tsp fenugreek seeds
1 small cinnamon stick, broken
  in small pieces
½ tsp ground ginger

Heat a heavy-bottomed skillet until hot. Add spices and seeds and dry-roast for 2 to 3 minutes, stirring, until they darken. Leave to cool. Grind everything together. Add the ground ginger. Store in an air-tight jar for up to 3 months.

CAJUN SEASONING

Cajun and Creole cooking is now widely known, having spread from Louisiana. There are lots of commercially made seasoning blends, all varying in flavor; most used dried onion and garlic, which give a finer texture than fresh ingredients, but if you prefer, replace the dried onion and garlic powder with a shallot and a garlic clove. This mixture is best used freshly made.

81

2 tsp paprika
2 tsp dried garlic powder
2 tsp dried onion powder
½ tsp salt

½ tsp ground cumin
½ tsp cayenne pepper
½ tsp ground black pepper
1 tsp dried thyme

Mix all the ingredients together and use as required.

COCONUT-SHRIMP CURRY

This dish of large tiger prawns or jumbo shrimp cooked gently in a rich coconut sauce flavored with a mouth-watering blend of chili, lemongrass, galangal, and cilantro is ideal served with plain boiled rice in individual bowls. Although there are lots of ingredients, the method is very simple and the result is delicious and worth the effort.

SERVES 2

2 tbsp vegetable oil
1 garlic clove, finely chopped
1 cup canned coconut milk
2 tbsp fish sauce (nam pla)
1 tsp light brown sugar
12 large raw tiger prawns or jumbo shrimp, shelled leaving tails intact, and deveined

½ cup fresh cilantro leaves and roots chopped separately
4 kaffir lime leaves, finely chopped, or finely grated peel of 1 lime
1 tsp coriander seeds, crushed
½ tsp ground cumin
½ tsp ground white pepper
1 tsp salt

GREEN CURRY PASTE
2 fresh green chilies, seeded and chopped
1 lemongrass stalk, trimmed and chopped
2 shallots, chopped
4 garlic cloves, chopped
1-inch piece of fresh galangal, peeled and chopped

TO SERVE
Boiled rice
Fresh red chilies, seeded and chopped
Chopped fresh cilantro
Flaked coconut

First make the paste. Put all the ingredients, except the cilantro leaves, in a mortar and pestle or a small food processor or mill. Grind into a rough paste; set aside.

Now make the rest of the dish. Heat the oil in a large skillet or wok. Add the garlic and fry for 2 to 3 minutes, until golden brown. Add the curry paste and stir to mix it with the garlic. Pour in half the coconut milk, the fish sauce, and the sugar, stirring well until the mixture thickens.

Add the prawns or shrimp and cook until they begin to turn opaque. Then add the remaining coconut milk and continue to cook, turning the prawns in the sauce, until they are cooked through. Serve in bowls, spooned over boiled rice, garnished with chopped cilantro leaves, red chili, and flaked coconut.

BROILED SHRIMP *with* PIRI-PIRI

Piri-piri sauce, a fiery condiment flavored with red chilies and garlic, is popular in Portugal. It is served in this recipe as a dipping sauce to accompany large tiger prawns or jumbo shrimp. A crisp green salad is the perfect complement. The sauce keeps well and, once made, it should be refrigerated, sealed, for up to a month; the flavor will develop more as time goes on. It is also an excellent accompaniment for barbecued pork and chicken.

SERVES 4

12 large raw tiger prawns or jumbo shrimp
3 garlic cloves
2 tbsp olive oil
2 tbsp chopped fresh parsley and lemon wedges, to serve

PIRI-PIRI SAUCE
3 red chilies
1 tsp coarse sea salt
⅔ cup olive oil
¼ cup red-wine vinegar

First prepare the prawns or shrimp. Rinse them and pat them dry with paper towels. Place them in a shallow dish. Crush the garlic cloves and mix with the oil. Pour over the prawns or shrimp, cover, and refrigerate overnight.

Meanwhile, make the sauce. Discard the stems from the chilies and then chop them, with their seeds. Put them in a small screw-topped jar with the salt, oil, and vinegar. Seal, shake well, and store at room temperature for at least 30 minutes for the flavor to develop; it will keep for up to a month in the refrigerator.

The next day, heat the broiler to medium. Drain the prawns, put on the broiler rack, and broil for 4 to 5 minutes, turning and basting with the garlic-oil marinade, until the prawns are cooked through. Alternatively, cook the prawns or shrimp on the barbecue.

Serve the prawns sprinkled with chopped parsley and accompanied by lemon wedges. Serve the *piri-piri* sauce in a bowl and dip the prawns in it.

83

Pomanders

Pounded spices, dried herbs, aromatic resins, wine, honey, and sometimes crushed precious stones have all been ingredients of the pomander, a portable scented ball used to bring fragrance to the home and to guard against infections when outdoors.

Pomanders were probably first used by the ancient Greeks and Romans. The Roman physician Pliny, writing in A.D. 1 described one containing cinnamon, cassia, calamus, cardamom, balm, marjoram, myrrh, saffron, wild vine, and betel nut. These were pounded to a stiff paste with wine and honey, molded into a ball, and enclosed in a gold or silver case, which was studded with jewels and pierced with holes to allow the scent to come through.

The name pomander comes from *pomme d'ambre*, meaning "apple of amber": apple because of the shape, and amber because of the color and also because early pomanders contained ground amber and other gemstones.

The type of pomander described by Pliny was familiar in Europe during the 14th and 15th centuries, but it was in the 16th century when they were most popular. At that time,

A Sleeping Apple

An apple to make one sleep is made of all these: Opium, mandrake, juyce of hemlock, henbane seed, wine lees, to which must be added musk that by the scent it may provoke him that smels unto it. Make a ball as big as a man may grasp in his hand; by often smelling to this it will cause him to shut his eyes and fall asleep.

DR. MATHIAS, 16TH CENTURY.
QUOTED BY MRS. C.F. LEYEL IN *THE MAGIC OF HERBS*, 1926.

a pomander hung in every room in the houses of the wealthy, and both women and men frequently carried jeweled pomanders around their necks or hanging from belts or girdles. The pomander was held to the nose when the carrier was traveling through a poor area where disease was common, and also when in contact with anyone who was sick. Elizabeth I received a "faire gyrdle of pomanders" as a present from a courtier. This can still be seen at Burghley House, in Cambridgeshire, England, and consists of six silver segments which open out like an orange, grouped around a central core and held in place by a silver ring. Each segment was filled with a different perfume.

Alongside jeweled cases and silver representations of fruit an alternative method had developed of hollowing out a real fruit, such as an apple or an orange, filling it with a spice mixture, and hanging it up to dry. Cardinal Wolsey (*c.* 1475–1530) was known for his orange and spice pomanders, which he carried when visiting the sick. The orange stuck with cloves that is today's most familiar form of pomander is a direct descendant.

Cardinal Wolsey, chancellor to King Henry VIII of England, is said to have been one of the first people to carry a fruit pomander.

Making a Pomander

Equipment

spoon
small bowl
fine skewer or toothpick
pastry brush
small paper bag
narrow Sellotape
ribbon and thread (optional)

Ingredients

fruit (orange, lime, lemon, or apple)
1 tbsp powdered orris root
*1 tbsp ground spices (choose the spice to suit your fruit: for
example, cloves for an apple; cinnamon for an orange;
cardamom for a lime; nutmeg for a lemon. Allspice and
coriander can also be used. The spices can be single or
mixed; or use a store-bought blend.)*
1 ounce cloves (good quality with large heads)

Method

In a small bowl, mix together the orris root and
ground spice(s). If you are using citrus fruits, gently
squeeze them with your hands to soften the skin and
make it easier to insert the cloves. Before making
holes for the cloves, decide how you want to display
your pomanders: hung by ribbon or in a net bag, or
placed in open bowls. If you intend to use ribbon,
mark the space for this with your first lines of cloves
or begin by sticking a cross of tape around the fruit
where the ribbon will go. Pierce the fruit with the
skewer or toothpick and push in the cloves,
distributing them in an even pattern over the fruit and
leaving the space of a clove head around each one.
This allows for the fruit to shrink slightly
as it begins to dry.
When the fruit is covered to your requirements,
remove the tape. Pat the mixture of orris root and
spice into every part of the surface. Put the pomander
into a paper bag together with any remaining spice
mixture. Leave it to dry in a cool, dry, airy room,
turning it every other day and making sure that it
remains coated in the spice mixture. Drying will take
from one to three months, depending upon the
atmosphere of the room and the weather conditions.
When a fruit is completely dry, it will be brown color
and will sound hollow when it is tapped.
Brush all the spices off the pomander with a pastry
brush. If you are using ribbon, wrap a strip around
the spaces between the cloves, stitching the ends
together at the top and bottom of the fruit. Sew on a
loop for hanging.

*Once you have mastered the basic method, you can
make pomanders with a variety of spices. These
pomanders have been made with spices such as star
anise, mixed peppercorns, cloves, and nutmegs.*

Pomander

*Take gum benzoin 2 drachms; storax and labdanum
(laudunum) 1 drachm; cedar bark, thin rind of orange and
lemon, rose leaves, rosemary, red sandalwood, calamus, of
each half a drachm; cloves, cubebs, iris, of each two
scruples. Reduce all to a powder and make into a paste
with gum tragacanth steeped in orange flower or rose-water.
The mixture to be placed in a hot mortar with a teaspoonful
of orange flower or rose-water, one scruple of civet and half
a drachm of ambergris, and then incorporated well together.
When this is done, half a scruple of musk, thirty drops of oil
of lily of the valley, and ten drops of oil of cinnamon are to
be incorporated with it when cold.*

SIR KENELM DIGBY, *THE CLOSET OPENED*, 1668

FRAGRANT MUSSEL *and* BACON RISOTTO

Plump, juicy mussels are at their best in the winter months. This hearty combination is subtly flavored with the spicy seeds of coriander and celery and has the golden glow of saffron. The rice used in this recipe is an Italian short-grain rice called arborio, which swells and softens on cooking and absorbs all the flavors of the dish. Accompany the risotto with warmed ciabatta bread and a glass of fresh, dry, Italian white wine.

SERVES 4

2 pounds fresh mussels
1 tbsp olive oil
4 slices Canadian bacon,
 rinded and finely chopped
1 red onion, finely chopped
1 garlic clove, crushed
2 celery sticks, finely chopped
1 tbsp lemon juice
4 tomatoes, peeled and chopped
1½ cups arborio rice
⅔ cup dry white wine

2 cups fish stock
1 bay leaf
1 tsp coriander seeds, crushed
1 tsp celery seeds
Large pinch of saffron
Salt and freshly ground black
 pepper
2 tbsp chopped fresh parsley
Chopped celery leaves, to
 garnish

First prepare the mussels. Discard any that are damaged or broken or do not close when tapped. Rinse them thoroughly under cold running water to wash out any sand. Scrape away any barnacles and seaweed and pull off the fibrous beards; set aside.

Heat the oil in a large skillet or paella pan. Add the bacon, onion, garlic, celery, and lemon juice and fry for 2 to 3 minutes, until just softened. Add the tomatoes and rice and cook, stirring, for 2 minutes longer, until the rice becomes opaque. Pour in the wine and continue stirring for 5 minutes or until the wine has been absorbed.

Pour in the stock and add the mussels, bay leaf, coriander and celery seeds, and saffron. Season with salt and pepper. Bring to a boil, reduce the heat, cover, and simmer gently for 20 minutes, until the mussels open and the rice absorbs all the liquid. Discard any mussels that do not open, along with the bay leaf. Stir in the parsley and sprinkle with celery leaves.

Tuna Steaks *with* Pepper Sauce

Tuna is a very "meaty" fish with a texture similar to tender beef. It is perfect for broiling or barbecuing. Here it is seasoned with mustard, paprika, and cayenne pepper before cooking and is served with a tangy pepper sauce that is flavored with harissa. Harissa is a hot, fragrant chili sauce from North Africa; it is easy to make your own (see page 80), or it can be bought. Squeeze fresh lime juice over the tuna steaks to serve and accompany with rice or couscous and a salad.

SERVES 4

4 fresh tuna steaks, each weighing about 4 ounces
Salt and freshly ground black pepper
4 tbsp Dijon mustard
2 tbsp dry white wine
1 tsp paprika pepper
½ tsp cayenne pepper
2 tbsp olive oil
Lime wedges, to serve

PEPPER SAUCE

3 tbsp olive oil
1½ cups sliced shallots
2 garlic cloves, finely chopped
2 tsp harissa (see page 80)
2 red bell peppers, seeded and sliced
1 can (14-oz.) crushed tomatoes
⅔ cup dry white wine
½ cup pitted ripe olives, sliced

Rinse and pat dry the tuna steaks. Season with salt and pepper on both sides. Mix the mustard, wine, and spices together. Spread over both sides of the tuna. Put in a shallow dish, cover, and chill for an hour.

Meanwhile, make the sauce. Heat the oil in a saucepan and gently fry the shallots, garlic, harissa, and red bell peppers for 5 minutes, stirring, until softened. Add the tomatoes and wine. Bring to a boil, and leave to simmer for 30 minutes, until thick and pulpy. Season and stir in the olives; set aside.

Preheat the broiler to medium. Put the tuna steaks on the foil-lined broiler pan. Drizzle with a little olive oil and cook for 5 to 6 minutes on each side, until golden and cooked through to your liking. Drain and garnish with wedges of lime and the sauce, served hot or cold.

Spice Quality and Packaging

OVER THE CENTURIES, SPICES HAVE BEEN CARRIED ACROSS THE WORLD ON THE BACKS OF DONKEYS AND PONIES, ON BOATS, AND IN PEDLARS' PACKS: JOURNEYS THEN TOOK MONTHS AND EVEN YEARS. NOW, AS SOON AS SPICES ARE READY, THEY ARE SHIPPED OR TRANSPORTED BY AIR FROM THEIR COUNTRIES OF ORIGIN TO REACH WAREHOUSES, MARKETS, AND STORES IN PEAK CONDITION.

In the late 19th century spices were sold individually in small boxes made from cardboard or thick paper with the label wrapped around the outside. Here are a selection of old spice manufacturers' labels (below, right, and far right).

In days gone by, there was often a risk of spices being adulterated for reasons that included masking bad quality and increasing the weight and bulk by adding water or floor sweepings. All adulteration processes were against the rules of the spice trading guilds, but they, nevertheless, continued. Today, spices are inspected at source and again in the warehouse. Immense care is taken over purity and at least one importing company has a system of steam pasteurization which produces a low microbiological count combined with the highest quality.

Packaging is also different today. If you were shopping in a medieval market, you would probably have bought spices loose by weight and carried them home in a leather or linen bag. In Victorian times, you might have been served from a large glass jar, and the spices would probably have been put into a piece of sugar paper for the journey home.

When individual packaging was introduced in the late 19th century, spices were sold in small boxes, made of thin cardboard or, more often, thick paper, with the manufacturer's label wrapped around the outside. Once the package was opened, the spices were exposed to air and moisture, because there was not any inner protection. The boxes that contain spices today are made of coated cardboard that will withstand a certain amount of damp, and the spices are enclosed in one or more bags, which can be folded or resealed. Cardboard tubs were popular in the first part of the 20th century, sometimes with metal tops and again with no real protection between the spices and the surrounding atmosphere. The expanding use of plastic improved these tubs, and they are still a popular form of packaging. The spices are protected by an uncrushable and impermeable layer and can often be shaken out through perforated tops. Many spices are now sold in small glass jars, which are convenient to use and which keep their contents in good condition. Even so, because these jars are often clear and expose the spices to the light, they should be kept in a dark cupboard.

The best way to buy spices is to begin with a supply in glass jars and then to buy refills that come in packets or in sealed plastic bags. However, be sure to use the spices in the jar before you put the new ones in—otherwise you will accumulate a layer of stale spices in the bottom of the jar.

THE ORIENT FINEST GROUND CINNAMON

1 oz. 28 grm.

ANGLO INDIAN PICKLE

Prepared by E.LAZENBY & SON Lᵈ LONDON. ENGLAND.

DR MORSE'S INDIAN ROOT PILLS.

★ COMSTOCK'S ★ DEAD SHOT WORM PELLETS

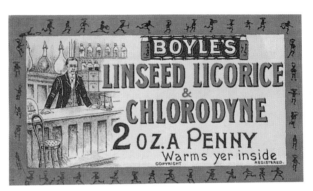

BOYLE'S LINSEED LICORICE & CHLORODYNE 2 OZ. A PENNY

Warms yer inside

COPYRIGHT   REGISTERED

Established 1855.

Gold Medal HIGHEST AWARD   Gold Medal PURITY AND QUALITY

Trade Mark

GUARANTEED the pure product of the Sugar Cane by distillation

STANDARD JAMAICA RUM

The Finest Rum Imported

TURNBULL,

51 High St. HAWICK. Scotland

MEXICANO APERITIVO PRODOTTO DA P.ROSSI.TORINO

A BASE DI VINO

MEXICANO APERITIVO ROSSI TORINO

PAOLO

GENUINE MADRAS CURRY POWDER

Prepared and Guaranteed by P. VENCATACHELLUM S. LOGANATH, MADRAS.

TO MAKE A REAL INDIAN CURRY

Use GENUINE MADRAS CURRY POWDER

THE BEST IS THE P. VENCATACHELLUM S. LOGANATH. "PAVASAL" BRAND

Sole Agents :— J. A. Sharwood & Co. Ltd. London. E.C.3.

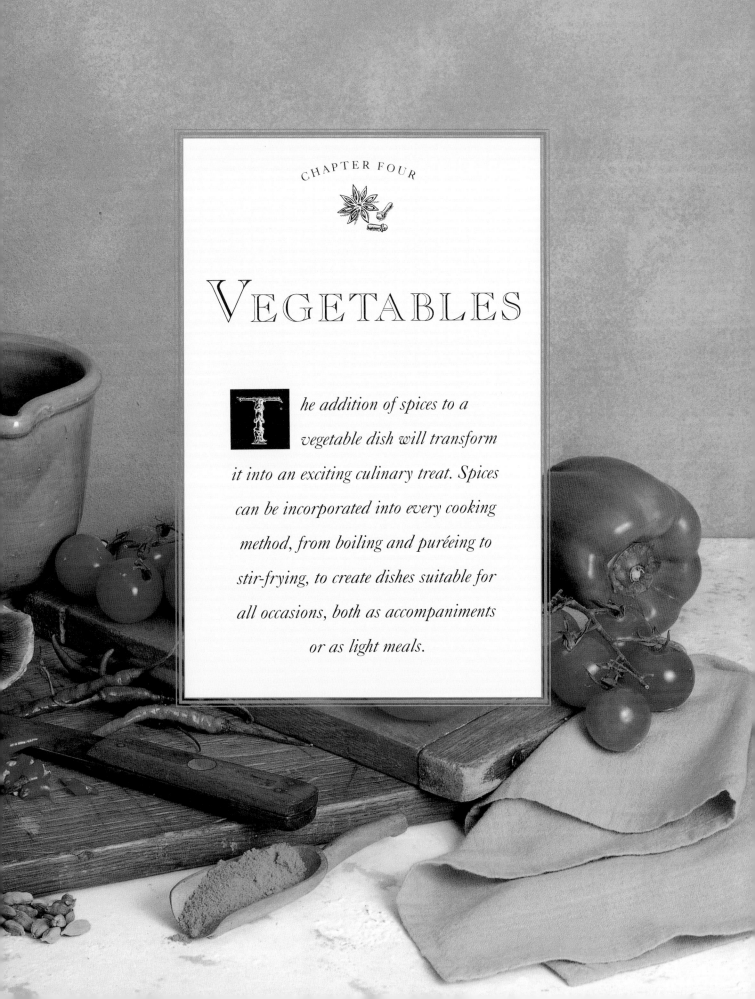

CHAPTER FOUR

VEGETABLES

The addition of spices to a vegetable dish will transform it into an exciting culinary treat. Spices can be incorporated into every cooking method, from boiling and puréeing to stir-frying, to create dishes suitable for all occasions, both as accompaniments or as light meals.

VEGETABLES

Every vegetable, however it is cooked and whatever it is served with, benefits from a little carefully chosen spice. Stir-fried vegetables or noodles can be flavored with the classic Chinese seasoning five-spice powder (a fragrant mixture of star anise, fagura, fennel, cinnamon, and cloves), or lightly flavored with a selection of coriander seeds, mustard seeds, and gingerroot. Creamy, puréed root vegetables are enhanced by the addition of black pepper, ground ginger, and freshly grated nutmeg. Spices add zest to dishes made from mild-flavored dried vegetables, such as chana dal or split peas. Rice and potatoes can be transformed by spices to make both fiery and subtle dishes. The Mexican dish Arroz Verde, *or "green rice," is perfect for pepper and chili lovers.* Gobi Aloo *is a delicately spiced Indian caulifower and potato dish flavored with a blend of spices and a hint of coconut.*

Nature morte de légumes et de fruits, *Jean-Jacques Spoede, 1725.*

MILANESE RISOTTO

Risotto alla Milanese is an Italian classic. The saffron is prominent, making the risotto rich, golden and fragrant—perfect accompaniment to an Italian meal. Saffron is the most expensive spice in the world but a small amount will flavor a large dish and color it a brilliant gold. Saffron is highly aromatic and has a bitter "flowery" taste. Serve this risotto as an accompaniment or for supper, with crusty bread and a salad.

SERVES 4

5 cups vegetable stock
4 tbsp butter
1 onion, finely chopped
1 garlic clove, crushed
Generous 1½ cups arborio
    (risotto) rice
Saffron strands
Salt and freshly ground white
    pepper
¾ cup freshly grated Parmesan
    cheese

Pour the stock into a saucepan and bring to a boil. Reduce the heat to maintain a gentle simmer.

Meanwhile, melt 4 tablespoons of the butter and gently fry the onion and garlic for 2 to 3 minutes, until softened but not browned. Stir in the rice and cook, stirring, for 2 minutes, until the rice is well coated in butter.

Add a ladleful of stock and cook gently, stirring, until it is absorbed. Continue to ladle the stock into the rice, until half the stock is used and the rice becomes creamy. Sprinkle in a pinch of saffron strands and season with salt and pepper.

Continue adding the stock until the risotto becomes thick, but not sticky. This will take about 25 minutes and shouldn't be hurried.

Just before serving, carefully stir in the remaining butter and the Parmesan cheese.

ARROZ VERDE

A Mexican dish which translates as "green rice." It is perfect for pepper and chili lovers, and is flavored with ground coriander and cinnamon. It can be served on its own as a main meal or as an accompaniment to a casserole. Be careful when preparing chilies: do not touch your face or eyes because the juice can be an irritant. Wash your hands immediately after handling chilies.

SERVES 4

2 tbsp vegetable oil
1 large onion, finely chopped
1 garlic clove, crushed
2 large green bell peppers,
    seeded and chopped
2 fresh green chillies, seeded
    and finely chopped
1 tbsp ground coriander
1 cinnamon stick
1½ cups long-grain rice
4 cups vegetable stock
1½ cups frozen peas
6 tbsp chopped fresh cilantro
Salt and freshly ground black
    pepper

Heat the oil in a large saucepan. Add the onion, garlic, bell peppers, and chilies and fry for 5 to 6 minutes, stirring, until softened but not browned.

Stir in the ground coriander, cinnamon, rice, and stock. Bring to a boil, cover, and simmer for 10 minutes. Add the frozen peas, bring back to a boil, replace the lid, and simmer for 5 minutes longer until the rice is tender and the liquid has been absorbed. Remove from the heat and leave to stand for 10 minutes.

Discard the cinnamon stick and stir in the chopped cilantro. Season well and serve.

95

Spinach *with* Cinnamon, Pine Nuts, *and* Raisins

Fresh spinach has a very delicate "earthy" flavor and is perfectly complemented by the woody flavor of cinnamon. Choose young spinach leaves for this recipe; they are tender and require little preparation. Always wash the leaves well, to remove any dirt. Serve this mouthwatering accompaniment with light meat or fish dishes, or as an interesting topping for pasta or rice.

SERVES 4

2 pounds fresh young spinach leaves	*1 tsp ground cinnamon*
4 tbsp butter	*1 tsp light brown sugar*
2 tbsp olive oil	*½ cup seedless raisins*
⅓ cup pine nuts	*Salt and freshly ground black pepper*

Rinse the spinach leaves several times. Pack them into a large saucepan while still wet. Cover and cook for 4 to 5 minutes, until just wilted. The spinach will cook in the steam from the water clinging to the leaves.

Meanwhile, heat the butter and oil. Add the pine nuts, cinnamon, and sugar and fry, stirring, for 1 to 2 minutes, until golden. Add the raisins and continue to cook for a minute longer, until the raisins are swollen.

Drain the spinach and mix in the cinnamon and pine nut mixture. Season well and serve at once.

Dal *with* Spinach

Chana dal are a small, brown Indian variety of the chick-pea; they are split and husked to reveal a small yellow pea that is part of the staple diet in India. In this recipe the dal are "roasted" with Indian spices: black mustard seeds, cumin seeds, ajowan seeds, and dried chilies, giving an earthy flavor. When served with rice or fried vegetables it makes a delicious main course, or it can be served as part of any Indian meal. If using older spinach leaves, cut off the thick stems before cooking.

SERVES 4

1 cup chana dal	*1 tsp salt*
1 tsp cumin seeds	*1 tbsp ghee or vegetable oil*
½ tsp black mustard seeds	*1 onion, finely chopped*
½ tsp ajowan seeds (or substitute dried thyme)	*4 tomatoes, peeled, seeded, and chopped*
2 dried red chilies, chopped	*1 tsp garam masala (see page 98)*
4½ cups water	
1 bay leaf	
1 pound spinach leaves, shredded	

Rinse the *chana dal* under cold running water, then dry them on a clean dish towel. Heat a heavy-bottomed skillet until hot. Add the dal, cumin seeds, black mustard seeds, ajowan seeds (or dried thyme), and chilies. Cook, stirring, for 4 to 5 minutes, until most of the dal turn orange-brown in color. The seeds will "pop" when hot.

Transfer the dal and spices to a large saucepan and pour the water over. Add the bay leaf, bring to a boil, and boil rapidly for 10 minutes. Partially cover and leave to simmer for an hour, or until just tender.

Stir in the spinach and salt. Cover and leave to simmer gently for 30 minutes longer, stirring occasionally.

Meanwhile, heat the ghee or oil in a small skillet and gently fry the onion for 3 to 4 minutes, until softened but not browned. Add the tomatoes and garam masala and cook for a minute longer.

Discard the bay leaf and stir the tomato mixture into the dal just before serving.

96

CURRY BLENDS

BASIC CURRY POWDER

A medium-hot blend that can be used in any dish that calls for curry powder.

6 dried red chilies, seeded and chopped
2 tbsp coriander seeds
2 tsp cumin seeds
½ tsp black mustard seeds

1 tsp fenugreek seeds
1 tsp black peppercorns
10 dried curry leaves
1 tbsp ground turmeric
½ tsp ground ginger

Heat a small, heavy-bottomed skillet until hot. Dry-roast the chilies, coriander, cumin, mustard, and fenugreek seeds and peppercorns over medium heat, until they darken slightly. Move the spices around to prevent their burning. Leave to cool. Grind the dry-roasted spices and curry leaves in an electric or manual grinder or with a pestle in a mortar. Stir in the ground spices. Store in an air-tight jar, in a cool, dark cupboard, for up to 3 months.

GARAM MASALA

This is the most common recipe for a blend used extensively throughout Uttar Pradesh and the Punjab. You can alter the quantities to suit the dish you are adding it to.

2 cinnamon sticks, broken in small pieces
3 dried bay leaves, crumbled
3 tbsp cumin seeds
2 tbsp coriander seeds

4 tsp black peppercorns
4 tsp cardamom pods
1 tbsp cloves
1 tbsp ground mace

Dry-roast all the spices, except the mace, as before, over medium heat for a few minutes until they darken slightly, stirring the spices to prevent their burning. Allow to cool before grinding and then mixing with the mace. Store as before.

MADRAS CURRY POWDER

A fragrant, hot blend which goes well with richer meats such as lamb and pork.

2 dried chilies, seeded and chopped
2 tbsp coriander seeds
1 tbsp cumin seeds
1 tbsp black peppercorns

1 tsp black mustard seeds
2 dried curry leaves
1 tsp ground turmeric
½ tsp ground ginger

Dry-roast the chilies, coriander, cumin, peppercorns, and mustard seeds as in Basic Curry Powder over medium heat, stirring for a few minutes until they darken slightly. Allow to cool. Grind the spices, with the curry leaves. Mix with the ginger and turmeric. Store in an air-tight jar for up to 3 months.

SRI LANKAN CURRY POWDER

A much more strongly flavored blend, which results from roasting the spices for longer.

2 tbsp coriander seeds	6 cardamom pods
1 tbsp cumin seeds	6 cloves
1 tbsp fennel seeds	6 dried curry leaves
1 tsp fenugreek seeds	1 tsp cayenne pepper
1 small cinnamon stick, broken in small pieces	

Heat a heavy-bottomed skillet until hot. Dry-roast the seeds, cinnamon, and cloves over medium heat, stirring, until dark brown. Leave to cool. Grind with the curry leaves and mix in the cayenne. Store in an air-tight container for up to 3 months.

WEST INDIAN CURRY POWDER

Curry powder was introduced to the West Indies by migrating Hindus in the 19th century. It is now widely used all over the islands.

2 tbsp coriander seeds	1 tbsp black peppercorns
1 tbsp aniseed	1 cinnamon stick, broken in small pieces
1 tbsp cumin seeds	
1 tbsp black mustard seeds	2 tbsp ground ginger
1 tbsp fenugreek seeds	2 tbsp ground turmeric

Dry-roast the seeds, peppercorns, and cinnamon over medium heat, stirring, for a few minutes until they darken slightly. Allow to cool. Grind and stir with the ginger and turmeric. Store in an air-tight container for up to 3 months.

THAI RED CURRY PASTE

A hot spice mixture that is used widely in Thai cooking. It is best prepared as required, but will keep for up to one month in the refrigerator.

1 tbsp coriander seeds	10 dried red chilies, seeded and chopped
1 tsp cumin seeds	
1 tsp black peppercorns	1 tbsp chopped cilantro roots
3 shallots, chopped	Finely grated peel of 1 lime
3 garlic cloves, crushed	2 tbsp fish sauce (nam pla)
2 lemongrass stalks, chopped	

Dry-roast the seeds and peppercorns over medium heat, stirring, until they darken slightly. Allow to cool. Grind to a powder. Mix with the remaining ingredients and blend to a paste.

99

GOBI ALOO

This cauliflower and potato dish is flavored with creamy coconut and a delicate blend of Indian spices, including turmeric, coriander, ginger, and cardamom and mustard seeds. Make sure you cut the cauliflower and potato into even-sized pieces to ensure even cooking. Serve this accompaniment as part of an Indian meal, with naan bread to mop up the sauce.

SERVES 4

1 tbsp vegetable oil
1 tsp black mustard seeds
seeds from 6 green cardamom pods
1-inch piece of fresh ginger, peeled and finely chopped
1 tsp ground turmeric
1 tsp ground coriander
1 cauliflower, broken into small florets

1 pound potatoes, peeled and cut into ½-inch cubes
2 tbsp gram (chickpea) flour (available from oriental grocery stores)
2 cups canned coconut milk
½ tsp salt
2 tbsp chopped fresh cilantro, to garnish

Heat the oil in a large saucepan. Add the mustard and cardamom seeds, and fry for 1 to 2 minutes, until they "pop." Stir in the ginger, turmeric, and coriander and cook for a minute longer, to form a paste.

Stir in the cauliflower, potato, and gram flour, until well coated in spice paste. Pour in the coconut milk, bring to a boil, cover, and cook gently for 12 to 15 minutes, until the vegetables are just tender. Season with salt and pepper. Spoon into a warmed serving dish and sprinkle with chopped cilantro to serve.

Dr Antonio Pigafetta

Doctor Pigafetta was the physician who sailed with Ferdinand Magellan in 1519. It was he who first recorded the finding of nutmegs and cloves on the Indonesian island of Tidore, and he kept a journal containing detailed descriptions of these discoveries. Here are two extracts:

The clove tree is tall and thick as a man's body … its leaves resemble those of the laurel and the bark is a dark colour … The cloves grow at the end of the twigs, ten or twenty in a cluster … When the cloves sprout they are white, when ripe, red, and when dried, black. They are gathered twice a year, once at the Nativity of our Saviour and the other at the Nativity of St John the Baptist … These cloves grow only in the mountains, and if any of them are planted in the lowlands near the mountains, they do not live … Almost every day we saw a mist descend and circle now one and now another of these mountains on account of which those cloves become perfect.

In that Island [Tidore] are also some nutmeg trees, the tree of which is like our walnut with the same leaves. And when the nut is gathered, it is as a small quince apple, having similar rind and the same colour. Its first rind is as thick as the green rind of our walnut, and under that is a thin loose rind, under which is the mace, very red and wrapped about the rind of the nut, and inside this is the nutmeg.

DR. ANTONIO PIGAFETTA, *JOURNAL,* 1519

CHAKCHOUKA

This is a Tunisian dish, now popular throughout the Middle East. It is an egg-and-vegetable dish flavored with harissa paste (see page 80), which is a hot blend of chilies and garlic, combined with the fragrant coriander, caraway, and cumin seeds. It can also be varied by adding sliced spicy sausages, such as *merguez* or chorizo. Serve as a light supper dish, with warmed Arabic or pita bread.

SERVES 4

4 tbsp olive oil
1 large onion, sliced thinly
2 red bell peppers, seeded and thinly sliced
2 yellow bell peppers, seeded and thinly sliced
4 tomatoes, peeled and quartered
Salt and freshly ground black pepper
1 tsp harissa (see page 80)
4 large eggs
1 tbsp chopped fresh mint

Heat the oil in a large skillet. Add the onion and bell peppers and fry for 5 to 6 minutes, until softened and golden. Add the tomatoes, seasoning, and harissa. Stir together, spread evenly across the pan, and break the eggs on top. Cook gently for 10 minutes, or until the eggs set.

Sprinkle with mint and serve straight from the pan.

Spices in Potpourri

Herbs and flowers alone are not enough to provide and maintain a long-lasting potpourri fragrance. Spices and spice oils are also needed to create an enriched and fixed scent.

Many of the potspourris sold today are produced by the so-called "dry" method, in which dried flowers and herbs are mixed with crushed spices, woods, and resins. Extra scent is given by the addition of essential oils. However, the name potpourri means "rotten pot" and this refers to the original method of making them used by the ancient Egyptians and Greeks. Sweet-scented petals were put into crocks with salt, buried in the ground and left to ferment. First they became very moist and then they dried, leaving a fragrant, long-lasting "cake" that was crumbled and mixedd with spices.

The same technique was popular in country houses in the 18th century throughout Europe, and was taken from there to the United States. In those days, it was usual for the lady of a wealthy household to have her own stillroom, where she dried herbs, distilled perfumes and flower waters, made fragrant preparations for the house, and mixed medicines. Almost every such household had its own recipe for potpourri, handed down through the generations.

A Quicker Sort of Sweet Pot

Take three handfuls of orange flowers, three of clove gillyflowers, three of damask roses, one of knotted marjoram, one of lemon thyme, six bay leaves, a handful of rosemary, one of myrtle, half one of mint, one of lavender, the rind of a lemon, and a quarter of an ounce of cloves. Chop all; and put them in layers, with pounded bay salt between, up to the top of the jar.

If all the ingredients cannot be got at once, put them in as you get them; always throwing in salt with every new article.

DOMESTIC COOKERY, 1834. QUOTED BY ELEANOR SINCLAIR RHODE IN
THE SCENTED GARDEN, 1931.

Making an Old-Fashioned Potpourri

To make potpourri in the original way, you will need access to large quantities of fragrant petals.

Roses: *These should form the bulk of the potpourri and can be the only flower used. Pick them on a dry day, just before they are full-blown, and carry them in an open basket, not a plastic bag.*

Other flowers: *Mix in a selection of available blooms, such as carnations, heliotrope, honeysuckle, lilac, lily-of-the-valley, lime flowers, mignonette, mock orange blossom, nicotiana, orange blossom, peony, pinks, stocks, violets, and wallflowers.*

Other ingredients

noniodized sea salt
crushed cinnamon and cloves
orris root powder to act as a fixative
grated lemon or orange peel

Equipment

a large earthenware crock or mixing bowl
weight to press the contents, such as a measuring weight,
or a bag of sugar on a plate or chopping board
bowls
spoons

Method

As soon as you get your roses home, remove the petals and scatter them in a single layer on especially made drying racks or on cooling racks covered with a layer of cheesecloth. Leave them in a warm, dry, airy place until they are half dried and the texture of soft leather. This will take about two days. Dry the other flowers in the same way.

Measure your petals by volume and put them into the crock or bowl. To every 4 cups petals add 1¼ cups noniodized sea salt, grated peel ½ orange or lemon, 2 teaspoons cinnamon, and 2 teaspoons cloves.

Put a weight on top of the contents and stand the container in a cool, dry place. This blend will suffice or you can continue adding petal and spice mixture throughout the summer as flowers bloom in your garden. When the last flowers are in, leave the container for two weeks. Check the contents. If a sweet-smelling liquid has formed in the bottom of the container, pour it off. (You can use it to scent your bath water. Replace the weight and leave the mixture for six weeks, checking once a week. After becoming very moist, the contents will shrink and dry and eventually become a sweet-smelling cake of petals. If you have used only red and pink roses, it will be pink. A mixture of colors makes it dull brown.

Break up the cake of petals and for each 8 ounces, add 1 ounce crushed cloves, ½ ounce crushed cinnamon, and ½ ounce orris root powder. Put the mixture into a plastic bag, seal, and leave for six weeks.

To use, transfer the potpourri to a container with a tight-fitting lid. Remove the lid when you want the scent to pervade a room. Provided you keep the potpourri away from direct heat and from damp, it should last for up to 10 years. If the scent diminishes after a time, revive it with extra spices, rose oil, a little brandy, or eau de cologne.

INDIAN-STYLE RICE *with* SPLIT PEAS

Although this dish is based on humble ingredients, it is very delicious and is often served as part of a lavish banquet. The Indian spices used, including turmeric, ginger, green chili, and garam masala, give a warming, comforting appeal. You can serve this with any meat dish, or with crisp salad vegetables and a yogurt and mint relish.

SERVES 6

⅓ cup skinned chana dal *or yellow split peas*	*½ tsp salt*
Generous 1½ cups basmati rice	*Cayenne pepper*
½ tsp ground turmeric	*2 tbsp ghee or unsalted butter*
6 tbsp vegetable oil	*Juice of 1 small lemon*
1 large onion, sliced into rings	*2 tbsp canned coconut milk*
2 garlic cloves, crushed	*2 fresh green chilies, seeded and finely chopped*
1-inch piece of fresh ginger, peeled and finely chopped	*2 tsp garam masala (see page 98)*
5 tbsp whole-milk plain yogurt	*2 tbsp chopped fresh cilantro*

Rinse the *chana dal* in cold, running water. Put in a bowl, cover with plenty of cold water; set aside to soak for 1½ hours. Meanwhile, rinse the rice in cold, running water. Put in another bowl and cover with cold water; set aside for 30 minutes.

Transfer the soaked dal and the liquid into a large saucepan and add the turmeric. Bring to a boil, partially cover, and simmer for 30 minutes, until just tender. Drain well to remove all cooking liquid.

Heat the oven to 325°F. Heat the oil in a large skillet and cook the onions, garlic, and ginger, stirring, for 5 to 6 minutes, until golden brown. Stir in the yogurt, 1 tablespoon at a time, allowing the liquid from the yogurt to evaporate each time. Stir in the dal, salt, and a pinch of cayenne, until well mixed.

Drain the rice. Put it in a saucepan, cover with water, bring to a boil and cook for 5 minutes. Drain well and spoon half into a baking dish. Spoon the dal over and top with remaining rice. Spread the ghee or butter over the top with the onion mixture. Sprinkle with lemon juice, coconut milk, chilies, and garam masala. Cover tightly with foil and bake for 30 minutes.

Sprinkle with the chopped cilantro and stir gently to mix before serving.

ORIENTAL STIR-FRIED VEGETABLES *and* NOODLES

This dish of crisp, oriental-style vegetables and noodles is flavored with the classic Chinese seasoning, five-spice powder—a mellow mixture of fragrant spices—star anise, Szechuan peppercorns, fennel, cinnamon, and cloves (see page 80). Serve this dish on its own as a vegetarian main meal or add strips of cooked chicken or pork for a nonvegetarian version. Use a wok or large skillet to cook the vegetables quickly so they retain their flavor and color.

SERVES 4

1 bunch of scallions	*2 tbsp light soy sauce*
4 carrots	*2 tbsp rice wine or sweet sherry*
1 mooli or white radish	*8 ouncesz egg thread noodles*
4 ounces snowpeas	*1 tsp sesame oil*
2 tbsp vegetable oil	*1 tbsp sesame seeds, toasted*
1 garlic clove, crushed	*1 tbsp snipped fresh chives*
1 tsp five-spice powder (see page 80)	*Soy sauce, to serve (optional)*

First prepare the vegetables. Trim the scallions and discard any outer damaged leaves. Shred the white and green parts finely into thin strips. Peel the carrots and mooli and slice into thin, matchstick-sized strips. Top and tail the snowpeas and slice into thin diagonal strips.

Heat the oil in a wok or large skillet. Stir-fry the garlic and prepared vegetables for 2 minutes. Add the five-spice powder, soy sauce, and rice wine or sherry and continue to stir-fry for 1 to 2 minutes longer, until the vegetables are just tender.

Meanwhile, cook or soak the noodles according to the directions on the package. Drain well and mix into the vegetables, with the sesame oil. Mix well and stir-fry for a minute longer.

Pile onto a warmed serving platter and sprinkle with the sesame seeds and snipped chives. Serve with soy sauce for dipping, if you like.

SPICY PAN-COOKED VEGETABLES

Liven up a selection of lightly flavored green vegetables with this mellow spice selection of coriander seeds, mustard seeds, and ginger. You can use any vegetable for this dish, but choose vegetables that all need to cook for the same length of time; otherwise part-cook some of them first. Serve these vegetables to accompany a Sunday roast or a rich, meaty casserole. You could also toss them into freshly cooked pasta for a vegetarian meal.

SERVES 4

8 ounces asparagus spears, cut into 2-inch lengths
4 ounces small broccoli flowerets
4 tbsp butter or margarine
1 tbsp vegetable oil
2-inch piece of fresh ginger, peeled and finely chopped
2 tsp coriander seeds, lightly crushed
1 tsp yellow mustard seeds
2 leeks, shredded
½ small Savoy cabbage, finely shredded
Salt and freshly ground black pepper
2 tbsp chopped fresh parsley, to serve

Bring a saucepan of water to a boil. Add the asparagus and broccoli and cook for 3 to 4 minutes, until just tender. Drain well; set aside to keep warm.

Heat the butter or margarine and oil in a wok or large saucepan. Add the ginger and coriander and mustard seeds and fry for a minute. Add the leeks and cabbage and stir-fry for 2 minutes. Add the asparagus and broccoli and continue to stir-fry for 3 minutes longer, until all the vegetables are just tender and heated through.

Season the vegetables well and stir in the chopped parsley. Serve as an accompaniment to a meat dish.

Spiced Ales and Beers

Before the widespread use of hops, spices and herbs were added to sharpen the flavor of ale and beer. They were put into the barrel with the newly brewed liquid, to impart their flavor as the liquid matured. Long pepper (a variety no longer consumed in the West) was a popular spice, together with nutmeg, cinnamon, and grains of paradise.
There were also special spiced drinks. A Bragot, flavored with honey, cinnamon, pepper, cloves, galangal, and ginger, was served on festive occasions in Britain. Aleberry, made with ale, a cereal mixture, and saffron, was thought to be good for invalids. Buttered ale was a favorite in the 17th century. The ale was boiled with butter, sugar and nutmeg and thickened with whole eggs or egg yolks. In Scotland, aleberry was thickened with oatmeal, and ale crowdie was made with oatmeal, treacle, and whiskey for the harvest celebrations.

SPICY PURÉED VEGETABLES

Puréed vegetables make a wonderful accompaniment for braised dishes that have lots of sauce or gravy. The vegetables are flavored delicately with ginger, celery seeds, nutmeg, and black pepper, so the spices complement the vegetables rather than dominate them.

SERVES 4

1 pound rutabaga	¼ tsp black peppercorns,
1 pound potatoes	crushed
1 pound celery root	½ tsp ground ginger
2 pounds spinach, shredded	2 tbsp snipped fresh chives
⅔ cup heavy cream	1 tsp celery seeds
1 stick butter or margarine	½ tsp grated nutmeg
Salt	

Peel the rutabaga and cut into 1-inch chunks. Put in a saucepan and cover with water. Bring to a boil and cook for 7 to 8 minutes, until tender. Drain well and return to the saucepan. Meanwhile, peel the potatoes and cook and drain as the rutabaga. Peel the celery root and cook and drain as the rutabaga.

Wash the spinach and pack it into a large saucepan while still wet. Cover and cook for 4 to 5 minutes, until wilted. Drain well, pressing to remove the excess water.

Working quickly, mash the rutabaga, potato, and celery root separately and then mash or chop the spinach. Heat the cream and butter or margarine until melted, and then divide between each saucepan. Mix well, then season the rutabaga with salt and black pepper; the potato with salt and the ginger and chives; the celery root with salt and celery seeds; and the spinach with salt and nutmeg.

Pile each vegetable into separate warmed serving dishes and serve.

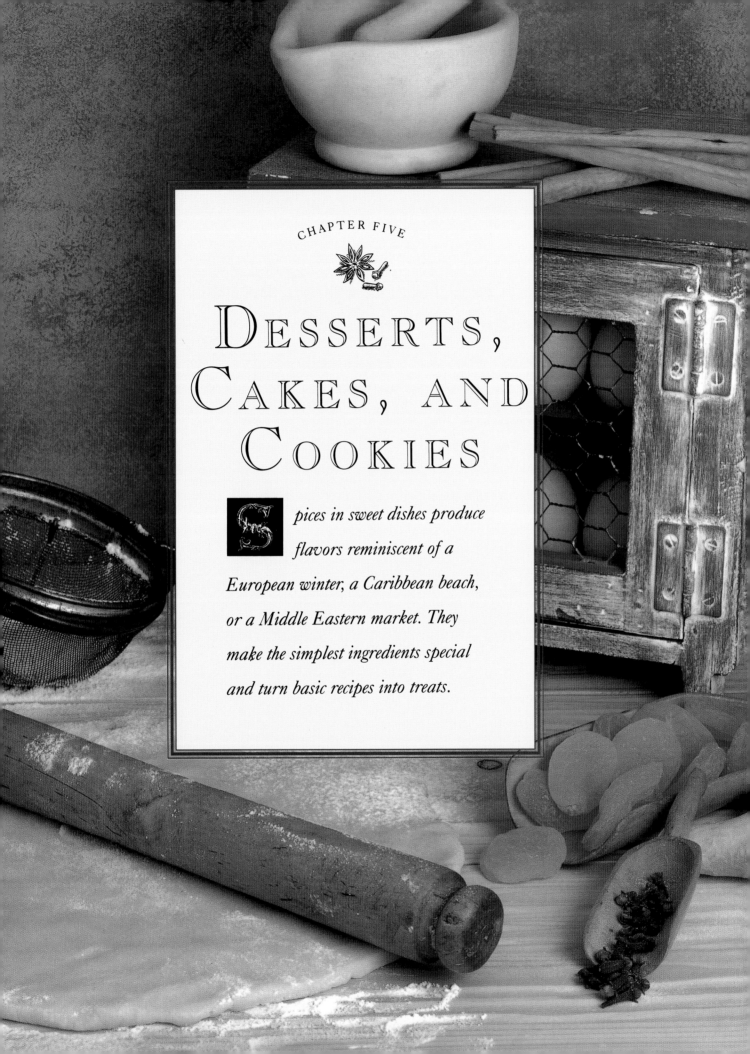

CHAPTER FIVE

DESSERTS, CAKES, AND COOKIES

Spices in sweet dishes produce flavors reminiscent of a European winter, a Caribbean beach, or a Middle Eastern market. They make the simplest ingredients special and turn basic recipes into treats.

DESSERTS, CAKES, AND COOKIES

The sweet spices, such as nutmeg, cinnamon, allspice, and cloves, come into their own for desserts. They can be used individually or in a blend, such as a favorite pudding spice mixture. Spices enhance homely dishes, such as Deep-Dish Apple Pie and Traditional Rice Pudding, and are essential to the character of Oriental Fruit Salad or Jamaican Bananas.

Cardamom pods give a whole new dimension to vanilla ice cream, and allspice added to Chocolate, Rum, and Raisin Fudge creates a very special sweet treat. Cinnamon Swirl Bread and Spiced Cranberry Muffins will fill hungry mouths on baking day, and you can reward yourself with a coffee accompanied by Chocolate and Vanilla Cookies.

Still life with candies and pottery, *J. van der Hamen y Léon, 1627.*

Deep-Dish Apple Pie *with* Cinnamon

Make the most of juicy cooking apples by baking them with a hint of cinnamon under a rich piecrust. Cinnamon has a deliciously sweet, woody aroma, and the flavor is intense, fragrant, and warm. This is a favorite dessert and there are many variations but, whatever the recipe, it is always served simply with vanilla ice cream, whipped cream, or custard sauce.

SERVES 6

PIECRUST
1¼ cups all-purpose flour
6 tbsp butter or margarine, cut in small pieces
1½ ounces blanched almonds, finely ground
2 tbsp sugar
5 to 6 tbsp milk

FILLING
2 pounds cooking apples
2 tbsp lemon juice
½ cup golden raisins
½ cup light brown sugar
⅓ cup slivered almonds
1 tsp ground cinnamon
1 small egg, beaten
1 tbsp brown sugar

Heat the oven to 375°F. First make the piecrust. Sift the flour into a bowl and mix in the butter or margarine until the mixture resembles bread crumbs. Stir in the ground almonds and sugar. Bind together with enough milk to form a firm dough. Knead gently on a lightly floured surface, until well mixed and smooth. Wrap and chill while preparing the filling.

Core, peel, and thinly slice the apples. Put in a large bowl and toss in the lemon juice to prevent them from browning. Stir in the golden raisins, sugar, slivered almonds, and cinnamon. Pile into a deep, 5-cup pie plate; set aside.

Roll out the dough on a lightly floured surface until 1 inch longer all around than the dish. Cut sufficient strips to line the outside rim of the dish. Secure on the dish with water. Brush the dough edge with beaten egg and top with the remaining dough. Press the edges together to seal and trim. Then press with a fork to make a decorative edge. Reroll out any trimmings and use them to decorate the top of the piecrust, if you like.

Brush the dough top with egg to secure any decorations and sprinkle with sugar. Make 2 slits in the middle for steam to escape. Bake for 55 minutes, covering with foil to prevent it from browning too much, if necessary, until golden and cooked through.

Vanilla *and* Cardamom Ice Cream

The addition of fragrant, lemon-scented cardamom transforms a traditionally flavored ice cream and gives it added zest. All the flavor in a cardamom pod is held in the small, hard seeds encased in an outer husk; they should be split to release maximum flavor. For perfect ice cream, do not allow the custard mixture to boil, or the eggs will scramble and the mixture will become lumpy. Serve this ice cream decorated with rose-scented geranium leaves and accompanied by crisp wafer cookies; it is also delicious with chocolate sauce.

SERVES 4

2 cups light cream
1 vanilla bean
6 cardamom pods, split

3 medium egg yolks
½ cup plus 2 tbsp sugar
⅔ cup heavy cream

Pour the light cream into a heavy-bottomed saucepan and add the vanilla bean and cardamom pod. Bring the mixture very slowly to a boil. Remove from the heat, cover, and leave to stand for 30 minutes.

Beat the egg yolks and sugar in a large bowl, until thick and pale. Reheat the cream to simmering point and gradually pour onto the egg mixture, stirring constantly. Strain through a fine strainer into a heavy-bottomed saucepan and stir over gentle heat, until the custard thickens enough to coat the back of a wooden spoon; do not let it boil.

Pour into a large heatproof bowl and leave to cool completely. Whip the heavy cream until it is just forming peaks. Fold into the cooled custard. Pour the mixture into a freezer container, cover, and freeze. Beat the mixture twice at hourly intervals. Cover, seal, and freeze for at least 2 hours longer. Stand at room temperature for 15 minutes before serving, to make sure it is just soft enough to scoop easily.

113

CHOCOLATE *and* VANILLA COOKIES

Vanilla is the perfect complementary spice for chocolate, and has been used to flavor chocolate since the late 16th century. Vanilla has a rich and mellow aroma and a fragrant sweet taste. Invest in good-quality vanilla extract rather than flavoring; the latter is synthetic and can leave a disagreeable aftertaste. These cookies are best eaten on the day they are baked. If you want, make a smaller batch of cookies and then freeze the unbaked cookie dough for up to three months.

MAKES 20

1½ sticks butter or margarine, softened
¾ cup light brown sugar
1 medium egg
2 tsp vanilla extract

1⅓ cups all-purpose flour
⅓ cup unsweetened cocoa powder
½ tsp baking powder
8 ounces white chocolate, broken in small pieces

Heat the oven to 375°F. In a mixing bowl, beat together the butter or margarine and sugar until light and fluffy. Beat in the egg and vanilla extract.

Sift in the flour, cocoa, and baking powder, and stir in the chocolate pieces. Pile plum-sized spoonfuls, well spaced, onto lightly greased baking trays. Bake for 15 minutes, until firm and pale golden. Cool on baking trays for 5 minutes then transfer to wire racks to cool completely. The cookies are best served warm.

TRADITIONAL RICE PUDDING

The simplest ingredients combine in this recipe to form a rich, creamy rice pudding, flavored with the traditional sweet spices of vanilla and nutmeg. Using whole spices in this pudding produces a strong, deep flavor. It is delicious served cold but can also be served hot, by heating gently after the cream is added, and sprinkling with nutmeg to serve. Accompany with dried fruit compote or with a hot cherry sauce for a satisfying pudding.

SERVES 4

2½ cups milk
½ cup short-grain pudding rice
1 vanilla bean
1 tbsp sugar

½ cup golden raisins
2 tbsp sweet sherry
1½ cups heavy cream
¼ tsp grated nutmeg

Pour the milk into a saucepan. Add the rice and vanilla bean. Bring slowly to a boil, then simmer gently for 20 minutes, until the rice is soft and has absorbed the milk.

Stir in the sugar, golden raisins, and sherry. Cover loosely; set aside to cool. Discard the vanilla bean.

Stir in the cream and transfer to a serving dish. Sprinkle with freshly grated nutmeg and chill for 2 hours to let the flavors develop before serving.

DRINKS

CHILI VODKA

A warming combination of vodka spiked with red chilies to take the chill away; it is also said to be good for head colds.

2 fresh red chilies   *1 bottle of vodka*

Rinse the chilies and prick them all over with a fork. Push them into the bottle of vodka. Seal and leave to infuse overnight. Strain the vodka and keep in the freezer. Serve ice cold.

MULLED WINE

A traditional, warming cup, often served around Christmas. It is a sweet, deliciously warming drink, flavored with ginger, cloves, cinnamon, and nutmeg.

SERVES 8

1 piece of dried gingerroot   *1¼ cups water*
6 cloves   *1 cup light brown sugar*
1 cinnamon stick, broken   *2½ cups red Bordeaux wine*
¼ tsp grated nutmeg
1 orange, scrubbed and sliced

Put the spices, sugar, and half the orange in a saucepan and pour in the water. Bring to a boil, then simmer for 5 minutes, remove from the heat, and leave to cool for an hour. Just before serving, strain the sugar liquid and return to the pan. Pour in the wine, and heat gently—do not boil. Serve in heatproof glasses or small mugs with the remaining orange slices floating on top.

SPICY RASPBERRY RATAFIA

"Ratafia" is the name for a cordial made by steeping fruit or herbs in brandy. Serve as an after-dinner digestive.

2 pounds raspberries, rinsed
2½ cups brandy
1 vanilla bean

6 coriander seeds, lightly crushed

Put the raspberries in a large, clean bottle or jar and pour in the brandy. Add the spices, seal and leave on a sunny windowsill or in the airing cupboard for a month. Strain through muslin and transfer to a clean bottle.

GINGER BEER

Called "beer" because it has a slight fizz, this drink is served all over the Caribbean It can be served hot or cold.

MAKES ABOUT 5 CUPS

4 ounces fresh ginger, peeled and chopped
5 cups water
1 cup sugar

Pared peel of 1 lime
4 cloves
1 small piece of cinnamon, broken

Put the ginger in a large saucepan and pour the water over. Bring to a boil, cover, and simmer for 30 minutes. Stir in the sugar until it dissolves. Remove from the heat and leave to cool. Add the lime peel, cloves, and cinnamon. Pour into a sealable container and chill for 2 days only. Strain and serve.

ARABIC ALMOND MILK

One of the most popular drinks in the Arab world, this is usually drunk during religious festivals. The cinnamon and orange-flower water give it a mild, sweet flavour. Serve poured over ice or diluted with iced water.

SERVES 8

4 ounces blanched almonds, finely ground
5 cups milk
1¼ cups water
½ cup plus 2 tbsp sugar

1 small piece of cinnamon, broken
1 tbsp orange-flower water or rose-water

Put the ground almonds in a large bowl and pour the milk and water over; set aside for an hour, stirring occasionally.

Line a strainer with cheesecloth and strain the almond liquid through, squeezing the ground almonds to extract as much milk as possible. Pour the milk into a large saucepan and add the sugar and cinnamon stick. Heat gently, stirring, until the sugar dissolves; do not boil. Stir in the orange-flower water or rose-water, remove from the heat, and leave to cool.

Pour into a pitcher and chill. Serve diluted with ice-cold water or ice cubes.

117

ORIENTAL FRUIT SALAD

For a refreshing end to any meal, try this mouthwatering selection of fruit flavored with the oriental spices ginger and star anise—the latter having a sweet, licoricelike flavor. Use any combination of your favorite fruits in this dessert. For a more filling dessert, spoon the fruit over sweetened cooked pudding rice, flavored with coconut milk or unsweetened shredded coconut.

Put all the fruit in a bowl and stir. Stir in the sliced ginger, ginger syrup, sweet sherry and star anise. Cover and chill for an hour to allow the flavors to develop.

Let the salad stand at room temperature for 30 minutes before decorating and serving.

SERVES 4

1 ripe mango, peeled, seeded, and sliced
1 papaya, peeled, seeded, and sliced
2 kiwifruit, peeled and sliced
8 ounces litchis, peeled and seeded

4 pieces of preserved ginger in syrup, thinly sliced, with 2 tbsp syrup
⅔ cup sweet sherry
½ tsp ground star anise
Sliced lime and fresh mint sprigs, to decorate

Saffron Cake

*Then there was a very excellent home-made
bread, and saffron cake, on which the Cornish
child is weaned and which he goes on eating
until the last day of his life.*

NATURALIST **W. H. HUDSON**, ON A VISIT TO
CORNWALL, IN ENGLAND, 1908

*Saffron Cake is a Cornish specialty, and
legend has it that the Cornish learned the recipe
from the Phoenicians, who came trading spices
for Cornish tin in ancient times. It is more like
a rich fruit bread than a cake, and is made by
infusing the saffron stigmas in warm water in
a covered jar. The water is then added to flour,
yeast, sugar, butter or Cornish cream, dried
fruits, and sometimes candied peel. The dough
is shaped into one large saffron cake or a
batch of saffron buns. They are a golden yellow
with a subtle, spiced flavor.*

GINGERBREAD

This is a real family favorite. It is a sticky, treacle-based
cake, flavored with warming, sweet ginger, and traditional
pudding spice: A blend of the sweet spices mace, nutmeg,
allspice, coriander, cinnamon, and cloves. This recipe calls
for ground ginger and preserved ginger, which are tender
pieces of ginger in sugar syrup. This version is frosted but
omit the frosting if you want to freeze the cake.
Gingerbread stores well: Wrap the cake in foil and store in
an air-tight container for up to a week.

SERVES 12

⅓ cup black treacle
⅓ cup golden syrup
½ cup Barbados sugar
4 tbsp butter or margarine
4 tbsp vegetable shortening
1⅔ cups all-purpose flour
1 tsp baking powder
1 tsp ground ginger
*1 tsp pudding spice (see page
    80)*

⅔ cup milk
*2 pieces of preserved ginger in
    syrup, drained and finely
    chopped*

FROSTING
1 cup confectioners' sugar
3 to 4 tsp water
*12 small pieces of preserved
    ginger in syrup, drained*

Heat the oven to 325°F. Grease and line 8-inch square cake
pan. Put the treacle, syrup, sugar, butter or margarine, and
shortening in a saucepan. Heat gently until melted together.

Meanwhile, sift the flour, baking powder, and spices into
a mixing bowl and make a well in the middle. Pour in the
milk and then stir in the melted treacle mixture and
chopped ginger until smooth and thick.

Pour the mixture into the prepared cake pan and smooth
the top. Bake for 50 minutes, or until risen and firm to the
touch. Leave to cool in the pan. Unmold and cut into 12
even-sized wedges and put the slices on a wire rack.

For the frosting, sift the confectioners' sugar into a bowl.
Add the water and mix to form a firm frosting. Spread over
each piece of cake and top with a piece of preserved ginger.
Leave to set for 30 minutes before serving.

BAKLAVA

This rich, sweet Middle Eastern pastry is often served with thick black coffee. Layers of wafer-thin pastry and a filling of chopped pistachios are baked with melted butter and the woody, sweet spice, cinnamon. The pastry is then soaked in a rose-water and lemon syrup, which is also flavored with cinnamon. Serve in small pieces as an after-dinner sweetmeat, or with coffee or tea for a mid-day break.

MAKES 24

1½ cups finely chopped
    unsalted shelled pistachio
    nuts
Generous 1¾ cups sugar
2 tsp ground cinnamon
1½ sticks unsalted butter,
    melted
18 sheets of phyllo pastry
    dough, thawed if frozen

SYRUP
¾ cup sugar
1 lemon, scrubbed
1 cinnamon stick
1 tsp rose-water

Heat the oven to 350°F. Mix together the pistachio nuts, sugar, and cinnamon. Brush a 7- × 12-inch baking pan with some melted butter. Lay a sheet of phyllo pastry dough in the pan, trimming it to fit if necessary. Brush the pastry dough with melted butter and continue this layering with six more sheets.

Spread half the nut mixture over and put six more buttered pastry dough sheets on top. Sprinkle over the remaining nut mixture and top with the last few buttered pastry sheets. Seal the edges firmly and bake for 30 to 35 minutes, until golden and crisp.

Meanwhile, make the syrup. Put the sugar in a saucepan. Pare the peel from the lemon, using a vegetable peeler, and extract the juice. Add the lemon peel and juice to the saucepan with the cinnamon stick, and heat gently until the sugar dissolves. Bring to a boil and cook for 2 minutes. Remove from the heat and set aside.

Once the baklava is cool, reheat the syrup and stir in the rose-water. Strain the syrup through a fine strainer over the baklava to soak the pastry; leave to cool. Cut into 24 wedges to serve. This is best eaten within a couple of days.

SPICED CRANBERRY MUFFINS

Muffins are an all-American favorite. In this recipe, the tartness of cranberries is complemented by the flavoring of sweet pudding spices, such as cinnamon, mace, nutmeg, coriander, and vanilla. If you prefer, use other dried fruit, such as raisins, golden raisins, or chopped dried apricot instead. Keep the muffins in an air-tight container for up to five days. They are best served warm.

MAKES 15

3¹⁄₃ cups all-purpose flour
4 tsp baking powder
2 tsp pudding spice (see page 80)
Salt
1 cup light brown sugar

1¹⁄₃ cups dried cranberries
1 tsp vanilla extract
2 medium eggs, beaten
1¹⁄₄ cups milk
1 stick butter or margarine, melted

Heat the oven to 400°F. Put 15 paper muffin cases in muffin trays that are at least 1¹⁄₂ inches deep.

Sift the flour, baking powder, pudding spice, and a pinch of salt into a bowl. Sift in the sugar and cranberries. Beat together the vanilla, eggs, milk, and melted butter or margarine. Make a well in the middle of the dry ingredients and gradually stir in the egg and milk mixture. Take care not to overmix, otherwise the muffins will not rise and will have a heavy texture.

Spoon the cranberry batter into the muffin cases. Lightly smooth the tops and bake for 25 to 30 minutes, until risen and golden. Serve warm.

JAMAICAN BANANAS

A dish with few ingredients that is also quick and easy to prepare. Bananas are a staple in the West Indies and are served in many ways. Here, allspice, a native spice, also known as Jamaican pepper, adds a fragrant and pungent taste to this sweet dish. Allspice has aromatic undertones of cloves, cinnamon, and nutmeg, so it is perfect for including in desserts. Serve these bananas simply with vanilla ice cream or whipped cream.

SERVES 4

4 large, firm bananas
4 tbsp freshly squeezed orange juice
1 stick unsalted butter
¹⁄₂ tsp allspice berries, crushed
¹⁄₂ cup dark brown sugar

4 tbsp dark rum
1 tsp grated orange peel
Orange slices and peel, to decorate
Vanilla ice cream or whipped cream, to serve

Slice the bananas in half lengthwise and toss them in the orange juice; set aside.

Melt the butter in a large skillet. Add the allspice and sugar. Stir over low heat until the sugar dissolves. Add the bananas and leave to simmer for 4 to 5 minutes, turning the bananas from time to time, until they become tender.

Add the rum and orange peel and heat through for a minute longer. Decorate with orange slices and peel and serve with ice cream or whipped cream.

CHOCOLATE, RUM, *and* RAISIN FUDGE *with* ALLSPICE

Fudge is a much-loved candy, and this recipe combines chocolate and raisins with the flavors of the Caribbean, dark rum, and allspice. You will need a candy thermometer for this recipe for a perfect result. If the fudge doesn't reach the correct temperature, it will crystalize, rather than be creamy smooth. If you prefer a firmer set, chill the fudge after cooling for about 2 hours.

MAKES 36 PIECES

3 tbsp dark rum	½ tsp ground allspice
½ cup seedless raisins	⅓ cup semisweet chocolate
2½ cups sugar	drops
1¼ cups heavy cream	¼ cup unsweetened cocoa
2 tbsp unsalted butter	powder

Put the rum and raisins in a small saucepan and heat gently for a minute, without boiling; set aside.

In a large, heavy-bottomed saucepan, put the sugar, cream, butter, allspice, chocolate, and cocoa. Heat gently, stirring, until the sugar dissolves and the chocolate melts. Bring to a boil and boil steadily, stirring occasionally, until a temperature of 240°F is reached (the "soft-ball" stage).

Remove from the heat. Add the rum and raisin mixture and beat until the mixture begins to thicken: this will take about 10 minutes of intermittent mixing. Pour into a greased 8-inch square pan and leave to cool and set. Mark into 36 squares and cut to serve. The fudge is best stored in a sealed container in the refrigerator for up to 2 weeks.

CINNAMON SWIRL BREAD

The warming, woody aroma of cinnamon is perfect in this breakfast bake. Serve warm and sliced, or lightly toasted, and spread simply with butter to savor the flavor. Try experimenting with your other favorite spices, such as ginger, nutmeg, or a blend, such as pudding spice (see page 80). To test if the bread is baked, see if it sounds hollow when tapped.

SERVES 8

1¼ cups white bread flour	1 tbsp sugar
½ tsp salt	1 small egg, beaten
6 tbsp butter or margarine, cut	2 to 4 tbsp lukewarm milk
into small pieces	1 tbsp ground cinnamon
1 tsp quick-rise dry yeast	5 tbsp honey

Heat the oven to 400°F. Grease and base-line a 7-inch straight-sided round cake pan. Sift the flour into a bowl with the salt. Cut in 4 tablespoons of the butter or margarine, until the mixture resembles fine bread crumbs. Stir in the yeast and sugar. Make a well in the middle and add the egg. Mix together, adding sufficient milk to form a firm dough. Turn out onto a lightly floured surface and knead for 5 minutes, until smooth and springy to the touch. Put in a greased bowl, cover with greased plastic wrap, and leave in a warm place for 45 minutes or until doubled in size.

Meanwhile, soften the remaining butter or margarine and stir in the cinnamon and 3 tablespoons of the honey to form a smooth paste.

Turn out the dough onto a floured surface, knead again, and roll it out to an 8- x 24-inch rectangle. Spread the cinnamon butter over. Roll up from the long edge to form a long roll. Coil the roll to form a spiral. Lift the coil into the prepared pan. Cover with greased plastic wrap and leave in a warm place for 45 minutes or until doubled in size.

Remove the plastic wrap. Bake for 20 to 25 minutes, until golden and brown.

Warm the remaining honey. Turn out the bread onto a wire rack and brush all over with the honey. Cool for an hour before serving, cut in wedges.

122

RICH FRUITCAKE

Here is a recipe for a melt-in-the-mouth moist fruitcake. The combination of dried fruits and nuts is flavored with sweet spices, such as nutmeg, ginger, and pudding spice. The cake is best made a month in advance, wrapped in baking parchment and foil, and stored in a cool, dark place.

SERVES 16

1 cup golden raisins

1 cup dried currants

⅔ cup seedless raisins

1 cup finely chopped no-need-to-soak dried apricots

⅓ cup chopped candied cherries

4 pieces of preserved ginger in syrup, drained and finely chopped

6 tbsp brandy

1½ sticks unsalted butter, softened

¾ cup packed dark brown sugar

3 medium eggs, beaten

1 tbsp black treacle

¾ cup plus 2 tbsp all-purpose flour

¾ cup plus 2 tbsp self-rising flour

Salt

1 tsp pudding spice (see page 80)

½ tsp grated nutmeg

1 tsp vanilla extract

⅓ cup blanched almonds, finely ground

Grated peel and juice of ½ orange

Grated peel and juice ½ lemon

In a large bowl, mix together the dried fruit, cherries, ginger, and 4 tablespoons of brandy. Cover and leave to stand in a cool place overnight. The next day, heat the oven to 275°F. Grease a deep 8-inch round cake pan with a removeable bottom. Line the bottom with 3 layers of baking parchment and the sides with 2 layers. Secure 2 sheets of brown paper around the outside of the pan with string, making sure the paper rises 1½ inches above the top of the pan.

In a large bowl, cream together the butter and sugar until light and fluffy. Gradually beat in the eggs, treacle, and all-purpose flour. Add the prepared dried fruit mixture and stir. Sift in the self-rising flour, a pinch of salt, and the pudding spice. Stir the ground almonds and orange and lemon peels and juices. Spoon into a prepared cake pan. Bake for 4 to 4½ hours or until a skewer inserted into the middle of the cake comes out clean. Leave to cool in the pan. When cool, remove from the pan and discard the lining papers. Make holes in the cake with a skewer and spoon the remaining brandy over. Wrap in fresh baking parchment and foil, and store in a cool, dark place for at least a month and up to one year. Spoon more brandy over every few weeks, if you like.

Spiced Candies

"Sugar and spice and all things nice."
ENGLISH TRADITIONAL NURSERY RHYME

UNTIL THE 16TH CENTURY, SUGAR WAS A LUXURY. IT WAS CONSIDERED PART OF THE "SPICERY" AND WAS KEPT LOCKED IN THE SAME CUPBOARDS. THE POOR COULD NOT AFFORD IT AT ALL. THE RICH REGARDED DISHES MADE WITH IT AS VERY SPECIAL. THE COMBINATION OF SUGAR AND SPICE IS, THEREFORE, AN OLD ONE.

The first spiced sweets were made in medieval times and took the form of comfits, which were small, spicy seeds with a sugar coating. Caraway comfits were scattered over roasted fruits, and they were eaten after meals as a treat and as a digestive. Red or white aniseed comfits were another favorite for sprinkling on apples, and they were also sometimes strewn over the sweet versions of pottages, which were dishes of a liquid porridge consistency, often based on almonds.

The habit of ending a meal with baked apples and caraway comfits lasted at least until the 17th century. In Shakespeare's *Henry IV Part 2*, Squire Shallow invites Falstaff to share the dish: "Nay, you shall see my orchard, where, in an arbour, we will eat a last year's pippin of my own graffing, with a dish of caraways."

From the 16th century onward, sugar became more available in many households, and preserving and candying were an essential activity for any housewife. Making comfits was a long and tedious business. It needed various spoons and ladles, a bowl to heat the sugar, which was suspended over a bowl that held hot coals, and another bowl to hold the caraway or aniseeds. The melted sugar was ladled over the seeds, which were stirred about to keep them separate. They were then left to cool and dry before the next coat of sugar was ladled in. Twelve coats of sugar were said to be the right amount for caraway and aniseeds.

When sugar became a readily available comodity, additional uses were found for

A selection of Dutch spiced chocolates flavored with nutmeg, cinnamon, pepper, and lemongrass.

Squire Shallow in Henry IV Part 2, *invites Sir John Falstaff to eat a "pippin... with a dish of caraways."*

Spiced candy is warming and soothing – a tasty treat that also eases sore throats. Parkinsons Lung Lozenges (above), aniseed balls (far left), and cough candy (left).

comfits. They were mixed into cakes as a replacement for dried fruits, and they were also eaten with very dry or sour wine to improve the flavor.

By the end of the 19th century, sugar was so widely available that candies were being made and sold especially for children. Aniseed comfits had become aniseed balls, a tiny seed, coated in a thick round ball of sugar, sometimes flavored with aniseed oil and given a brown outer layer. The candy was sucked down to the seed. In the 20th century, a direct descendant of the caraway comfit was the "gobstopper," a large ball about 1 inch across, often made up of different-colored sugar layers. Great fun was taking the candy out of your mouth to see what color it had become. Nestling in the middle was the caraway seed.

Also at the end of the 19th century, candy was made from pulled sugar. Some were just plain sugar and some were colored and flavored. Fruit flavors were the choice of many, but candy enhanced with spice oils was popular in the winter months to clear the head and keep away colds. There were red and white striped cushion-shaped candies flavored with clove oil; yellow twists with aniseed; and black ones with licorice. Cough candy was another variety. You can still find it, singly or in mixtures called "Winter Warmers," stored in large glass jars on the shelves of old-fashioned candy stores.

Gingerbread

It is said that the first gingerbread recipe was devised by a baker on the Greek island of Rhodes in about 2400 B.C. The ancient Egyptians also liked spiced honey cakes, and the Roman legions carried gingerbread to sustain them on long journeys. During the Dark Ages, when few people had access to spices, gingerbread was made in the monasteries. Bread crumbs formed the basis of a medieval recipe, which also contained ginger, pepper, saffron, and cinnamon, and was sweetened with honey. The mixture was pressed into a square mold and the result was a solid, spicy slab, which was often colored red-brown with powdered sandalwood and decorated with box leaves secured with cloves.

The large amounts of spices in gingerbread, and hand-decorating, made it expensive, but it was a favorite with the rich for centuries. During the 13th century, Holland exported it to various parts of Europe, including England and Scotland. Gingerbread lords and ladies were made for Elizabeth I of England to resemble her courtiers.

Today, gingerbread is mainly a tea-time cake in Britain and a dessert in the United States, but in Germany it remains a cake for special occasions. The German word for gingerbread is Lebkuchen. In texture it resembles a soft, light, thick cookies and it is baked in a variety of shapes. From these came the story of the gingerbread man. Lebkuchen are sold with or without a chocolate coating and are often decorated with piped sugar frosting. As gifts for weddings, birthdays, anniversaries, and christenings, they are piped with the names of the recipients or with sayings and phrases. Chocolate-coated Lebkuchen hearts are sold at beer and wine festivals. They are also a traditional lover's gift. The most spectacular Lebkuchen of all is the Lebkuchen Häuschen, or gingerbread house, which is made at Christmas.

GENERAL INDEX

INDEX *of* RECIPES

CREDITS

Key: *t* top, *c* centre, *b* below, *r* right, *l* left

AKG London 7*tr*, 9*tl*, 10*bl*, 11*cr*. 14*tl*, 17*bl*, 18*tc*, 22*tl*, 58*tr*, 79*tr*; Ann Ronan at Image Select 10*tl*, 13*cr*, 23*tl*; ET Archive 13*tc*, 14*br*, 15*br*, 23*cl*, 31*tr*, 32*bc*, 33*tr*, 46*bc*; Douglas Dickens 47*tr*; Harry Smith Collection 31*bl*, 66*bl*, 67*br*; Image Bank/Carlos Nevajas 30*tr*; Image Bank/Kay Chernush 32*tl*; Image Select 12*tr*, 31*tl*, 75*c*, 84*bl*, 124*bl*; Lush Ltd 18*br*; McCormick Foods 6*bl*; The Mansell Collection 13*bl*, 16*tl*, 20*t* & *b*; North Wind Picture Archives 6*tl*, 7*br*, 8*tr*, 12*bl*, 15*tr*, 23*br*; Robert Opie Collection 17*tl*, 46*c*, 66*tl*, 88, 89, 125*tl*; Phot/Nats Inc 67*tl*; Poseidon Pictures 8*bl*; Nicholas Devore/Tony Stone Images 24*tl*, 33*br*; Paul Chesley/Tony Stone Images 30*tl*; Visual Arts Library 9*bl*, 11*tl* & *bl*, 22*bl*, 37*c*, 55*c*, 93*c*, 111*c*.

All other photographs are the copyright of Quarto Publishing plc.

Quarto would also like to thank the following for supplying product photography: Lush Ltd., 29 High Street, Poole, Dorset, BH15 1AB, Schwartz Spices, Thames Road, Haddenham, Bucks, HP17 8LB and Tisserand Aromatherapy, Newtown Road, Hove, Sussex, BN3 7BA.

Gail Duff would like to thank the following people for their help in supplying information: Martin Muggeridge, Lion Foods Ltd., Astmoor, Runcorn, Cheshire and Philippa Yeoman, The Food and Drink Federation, London.

Index by Dorothy Frame